HOW TO KNOW WHEN YOU'VE GOT IT MADE

Other Word Books by the Same Author . . .

Help! I'm a Layman

Is There a Family in the House?

SHAPING A SUCCESSFUL LIFE

Ken Chafin

HOW TO KNOW WHEN YOU'VE GOT IT MADE

WORD BOOKS
PUBLISHER
WACO, TEXAS

HOW TO KNOW WHEN YOU'VE GOT IT MADE

Scripture quotations identified KJV are from the King James Version of the Bible.

ISBN 0-8499-0271-1
Library of Congress Catalog Card Number 81-51222

Printed in the United States of America

This book is lovingly dedicated to
MAE WORTHMAN, my mother,
and
W. P. and THELMA BURKE, my wife's parents,
the three of whom are a very vital part of
the support system of my life.

Contents

Preface

THIS BOOK WOULD have never been written had I not become totally disillusioned with all the definitions of success which I saw people using to measure their lives. But I'm not able to settle for pointing out the inadequacy without asking myself the question, "What does it really take to shape a successful life?" This book is the beginning of an answer to that question. This is not an autobiography on "how I built a successful life" because I am a fellow pilgrim living in the same world with the same pressures, temptations, frustrations, and dreams as everyone else.

I'm convinced that building a successful life is an option which is open to each of us, and *How To Know When You've Got It Made* is based on that premise. In so many areas of life, it seems for one person to win, someone else has to lose, but the shaping of a life is not a competitive affair. Instead, it's an emphasis upon personal wholeness. With that in mind, having a successful life is not defined in terms of material possessions accumulated, but in the ability to survive as a spiritual being in a materialistic society; it is not so much acquiring power and status which distinguishes us from others, as it is establishing a way of relating to people in a loving way; it is not so much learning how to be assertive, as it is learning to be a real person.

I would be untrue to my deepest feelings if I did not acknowledge my indebtedness to those who have been of particular help to me in the writing of this book. There were a lot of people who helped me move from that very rough first draft to the form in which it appears in this book. At our house my wife Barbara, in the midst of all her other responsibilities, did the first reading and styling suggestions. At my office Gail Askew and Jane Mahns typed the next two drafts. At Word Publishers Beverly Phillips got it ready for the printer after Al Bryant did a second reading of the edited book.

Most of all I am indebted to Editorial Director Floyd Thatcher for the page by page detailed counsel he gave me, for forcing upon me the discipline of rewriting, and for his great encouragement in the project. Working with him on the book was like being in a one-person seminar on writing. Behind all of these is that host of men and women whom I know and have known who are in the process of building whole, happy, and successful lives. I'm grateful to be the pastor of a great church which sees my writing as a valid part of my ministry with them.

How To Know When You've Got It Made is not based on some new or untried theory, but rather draws from some very old and fundamental principles of life and relationships which are rooted in man's best understanding of God and his Word. If they seem to be new and fresh, it's because they have been used so little in today's world. Nothing is suggested in the book which I have not seen modeled in the lives of countless individuals and which I am not presently trying in my own life. This is not a book of gimmicks, but a pulling together of some of the essential ingredients of a successful life along with some guidelines and practical suggestions and illustrations from the lives of others. The book can be read in a few hours, but putting it into practice will take a lifetime. If in the process of reading the book you get a little clearer idea of what your life was intended to be and begin to move in that direction, then that will be an adequate reward to me for writing it.

KENNETH CHAFIN
Houston, Texas 1981

1

How Do You Spell Success?

EARLY IN HIS college years, Dick Wilson got involved in a campus election and discovered that he enjoyed the political life. As a result, he switched from a major in business administration to political science, and though he didn't tell anyone at the time, he decided that one day he would be a United States Senator from his state. While still in college, Dick became active in his political party and attached himself to the campaign of every promising candidate. His brightness and drive attracted the attention of the congressman from his district, and upon graduation Dick served on his staff in Washington.

The electricity and glamour of Capitol Hill and the whole Washington scene created surges of determination which drove Dick toward success. But when he had learned all he could from that particular job, Dick went home to help his father with the family business. He took a job in the county junior college teaching political science and began to build a base for fulfilling his dream of becoming a United States Senator.

During the process of clawing his way up the political ladder, Dick served four uneventful terms in the state legislature, made an unsuccessful bid for the office of state Attorney General, and filled two terms as Governor before everything seemed right for the big step. After a vigorous campaign and a decisive election day victory, Dick was sworn in as United States Senator—almost twenty years to the day from the time he had promised himself, "I'm going into politics, and someday I will be a senator."

His first days were spent settling in, learning the ropes, and getting to know his colleagues. But when the honeymoon was over, Dick began to experience feelings of disappointment. When he mentioned this to the senior senator from his state, he was reassured, "You'll get over that feeling. You're just realizing that you've got to be around awhile to pick up significant committee assignments and collect enough seniority to have any clout. Just you wait."

His colleague's advice seemed to make sense, so Dick worked and waited. As his seniority built up with the passing of years, his committee assignments became increasingly prestigious. He exercised power that went way beyond his earlier fantasies. As a powerful senator, Dick maintained intimate ties with our country's leaders as well as many other prominent people across the world. But with all of his outward success and acclaim, he felt hollow and empty inside. While he had accumulated the trappings of power and success, he did not experience the anticipated sense of fulfillment that had dominated his dreams for so long. And in an effort to cope with his feelings of emptiness and confused hurt, he became an alcoholic.

A young entrepreneur, John Bradley, came to Houston several years ago, about the time I did. John was handsome, bright—the son of affluent parents. His father had wanted him to stay in San Antonio and run the family construction company to prepare for taking over the family's various businesses. But John wasn't interested.

When I first met him, he told me, "It took my dad till he was fifty-five to become a millionaire. My goal is to make a million bucks by the time I'm forty." Coupled with his determination was the knowledge that Houston's future would likely explode and develop opportunities beyond the imagination of most dreamers. So he applied his creative imagination and began to syndicate land deals in the fast-developing areas of the city. It was a high risk business, but he hit it at just the right time and made his first million at age thirty-six, four years ahead of his schedule.

It came as no surprise to me later when I learned that his early success did not bring him that anticipated sense of fulfillment. He decided that if acquiring one million didn't give him the feeling, maybe making several million would. So he moved back on the racing treadmill with his eyes on a multimillion dollar goal. Unfortunately, though, John is just setting himself up for a bigger letdown because the hunger that drives him so relentlessly has no relationship to the goals which he's set.

Dr. Bob Bradford is the senior minister of one of the largest, wealthiest, and most influential churches in America. He was reared by loving but poor parents on land they farmed for a share of the crops. Though Bob didn't seem to resent his circumstances, he longed for something better. When he finally left home to attend Teacher's College on a work scholarship, Bob knew he never again wanted to live on a farm. So he attacked his studies with such vigor that by the time he was a junior one of his teachers suggested that "with such a mind surely you're planning to go to graduate school."

While this went beyond his original dream, Bob decided to attend a theological seminary and become a minister—to the delight of his mother and to the disappointment of his father. He graduated with distinction and took his first church. As time passed, Bob sharpened and perfected his ability to communicate, fine-tuned his other skills, worked on the boards and committees of the denomination—all with the same intensity he had applied in his college and seminary years. Now, after working with six congregations in three different states over a period of thirty years, he is comfortably situated in what is considered by many to be the best and most prestigious church in his denomination. Bob has obviously come a long way from that boy on the tenant farm, but I happen to know that he still doesn't feel like he's "got it made." He has reached the peak of his professional career with only twelve years left until retirement, and he's bored.

I was introduced to Dick Freeman while he was Chairman of the Board of Tenneco, one of the great energy companies of the world. We shook hands and exchanged pleasantries. Later I sat at his table for a dinner honoring him for his support of a children's hospital in Denver, Colorado. I gave the prayer of benediction. And another time Barbara and I sat in his box at the rodeo. Beyond that, I had no other contact with him.

One night his secretary, who is a member of our church, called me at home and said, "Kenneth, I have a favor to ask of you. Mr. Freeman is in St. Luke's Hospital. He has cancer. Last night his doctors told him that he has less than a year to live. My boss is a strong man; he couldn't have done what he has if he hadn't been. But he doesn't have the resources for dealing with this. Would you go see him? Possibly he will let you help him."

That first visit is indelibly etched on my mind. His room was more like a sitting room with a hospital bed in it than the usual hospital room. It had a lived-in feeling. There were snacks on the tables, newspapers which had been read and laid aside, and folders on a number of the activities he had been involved with during his retirement years. His next big event was the Houston Stock Show and Rodeo of which he was the chairman. As I entered the room, I met and spoke briefly with two of Houston's civic leaders who were leaving. Then I walked to the foot of his bed and started to introduce myself. "Mr. Freeman, I'm . . ." I got no further when he interrupted, "I know who you are, but I'm not a Baptist." He spoke with a directness which characterized his relationships with people.

"I'm not hunting for someone to baptize," I responded. "Maritta told me about the report the doctors gave you last night. That's a pretty rough message for anyone to hear, and I thought you could use a friend. I'm here to offer my friendship during this time."

Almost before the last word was out of my mouth he said, "I'm going to whip this thing." He said it with such force that I knew if determination was all it took, he *would* whip it. "Good," I said. "Then I'll carry your things out of the hospital and help you celebrate." As we continued to talk, some of the bite left his speech, and he motioned for me to sit in the chair beside him. Finally, he told me that he had not slept at all since the doctors informed him of his condition and that he had spent the night replaying his life and thinking about it.

We talked for thirty minutes without his ever coming back to my offer of friendship. But evidently he had been thinking about it throughout our conversation because as I stood to go he thrust his hand out to me and said, "It's a deal." I prayed for him and left, but I knew I was now involved with one of the most remarkable persons I'd ever encountered and that both of our lives would be affected by this new friendship.

That first visit was on the Monday after Thanksgiving, but there were many more during the next several months. Our conversations were open and honest and covered a wide variety of subjects—some trivial, others of profound importance. As our friendship grew, a love developed between us that was deep and genuine. We helped each other. I helped him to understand about God's nature and his love, and he entered into a relationship with God which gave him more reason for living and less fear of dying. He helped me to see more clearly how easy it is to succeed beyond your fondest dreams and still not have it made.

One night when Mr. Freeman was in an expansive and philosophical mood he delivered a soliloquy which I suspect he composed and edited in his mind during the day and then saved for our conversation. It began with a recitation of what he and his wife Norma had when they started out. He told me about the struggle of his early years and the moves which brought him to the top of Tenneco. He described in graphic detail the wealth and holdings he had accumulated. And then he paused for a moment, looked off into space, and said quietly, "Kenneth, a man's a fool to spend his whole life building a great corporation and then discover—at age seventy, when he's about to die—what life is all about."

Most of us know people who seem to feel that the only satisfaction and meaning we get from life is found in the journey and not in the destination. I'm frequently around people who belittle what they've become and idealize the path which got them there. Their interpretation of life seems to reflect some of the cynicism found in the lyrics of the song Peggy Lee made famous in the

1960s, "Is That All There Is?" As I've listened to the song many times, I've come to believe that the devastating lyric isn't found in the song itself. Rather, it's the one which the composer left for the listener to add. The mood of the song assumes that the listener will add a silent but sad, "Yes. That's all there is." But the answer to the question is "No. There's more." The good news is that the purpose and meaning of our life can be known and experienced.

How can so many of us get caught in the trap of a success that is empty? The reasons, I believe, are as varied as people, but there are some unique signals which can alert us to possible answers. The most glaring signal is *aimlessness.* It is amazing how many people seem to meander through the daily routines of life without any carefully thought out plan. Frequently, we become so obsessed with the expediencies of the moment that we're unable to see much beyond the length of our shadows. We are caught up in a mad rush like a hamster running on an exercise wheel—frantic action but going nowhere.

I recall a very unhappy woman who said in desperation, "I'm just not getting anywhere with my life." And after that bleak admission, she went on to pour out her feelings of uselessness—her life was empty and without any sense of meaning and purpose. Finally, when she ran out of words, I asked, "Where would you like for your life to be going?" With a puzzled expression on her face, she stared off into space for several moments and then looked back at me with eyes that betrayed agitation and confusion. When she spoke, her voice was flat. "I really don't know," she responded with a haunting tone of resignation in her voice.

Our natural tendency is to compartmentalize life and focus on one part of it and not the whole. Then we cultivate that part and neglect the rest of life. We say to ourselves or to others, "What I'd really like to become is a successful______." Depending upon the person the blank could be filled with athlete, writer, homemaker, engineer, teacher, farmer, and so on. No matter what word you put in the blank, each area has its own criteria for success, its own disciplines, and its price. Only a few reach the top in any field, but those who do usually enjoy status, prestige, and sometimes money. I admire the discipline and the determination of anyone who succeeds in his or her profession.

It is a common experience in today's world, though, for people to make grand successes of their vocations and still be miserable failures as persons. The tendency is to give ourselves wholly to a job or profession and ignore our personal life—to ignore marriage and family, and relationships with other people. Actually his happens to all kinds of people. But it has happened to enough people in high and visible places to remind us of the danger to us all. There's Wilbur Mills who, as Chairman of the House Ways and Means Committee, was considered one of the most powerful men in the United States. But his life was so out of control that he relied on alcohol to give him meaning, and on a striptease dancer to provide a relationship.

While there are persons of integrity in both government and business, we have been exposed during the last few years to the ravages of broken careers where ambition has not been tempered by integrity and character. This is always a danger to any of us who let our lives become fragmented so that we forget some of the indispensable parts of life.

Another false definition of success and personal fulfillment is found when we measure life in terms of what we don't have. If we are poor, we feel money is the answer. If we think we've been disenfranchised, we turn our energy to obtaining equality. If we are stuck in one place, we think moving is the answer. We mistakenly define our lives in terms of felt needs. In the midst of the civil rights struggles I'm sure that many people felt "once the schools are open, once we can vote without fear, once we can get a job as a person and not as a certain race, and once we can buy a home anywhere—we'll be happy." But the problem with this concept is that the racial majority already has what the minority is fighting for. However, the majority doesn't feel all that fulfilled. When we define fulfillment in terms of what we don't have or haven't experienced, we are setting ourselves up for bitter disappointment.

A problem which I consider to be just as serious as measuring life in terms of what we don't have is that of buying into an outward *image* of success. Observe the blatant hucksterisms of television: which toothpaste creates sex appeal, which automobile denotes power, which pair of blue jeans marks a teenage girl as better than her classmates. We are bombarded on every channel with the notion that if we acquire the right objects, their magic will somehow wear off on us; we will actually become the bright, attractive individuals who appear with the products. Unfortunately, this superficial gloss—the accumulation and display of possessions—seems to be the new definition of success.

I've lived long enough now to see this definition applied in interesting ways. When I began graduate school in Fort Worth, Texas, in the early 1950s, there was a country and western entertainer who was working in the honky-tonks along the Jacksboro highway. He played the guitar and sang, but he also wrote music and sent it to Nashville in hopes that some star would record one of his songs. The places he played in were so rough they had to put chicken wire up in front of the band to protect them from objects thrown by the customers. He hardly made enough money to buy strings for his guitar. Almost anyone who knew him at that time would have said that he was a failure. It seemed a shame for a grown man to waste his time and talents that way.

Today that same man is considered the high priest of progressive country music. He has countless gold and platinum records, has been the recipient of country music's most coveted awards, and his fans will fill any place that books him. In many ways he has changed very little during the past twenty-five years. His dress, lifestyle and friends are the same. The music he writes develops the same themes. The one overwhelming difference is that he has been able to use his talent to generate an enormous amount of money and has translated that money into power and status. Now people call him a success.

A lot of bad things happen in a society which closely identifies the worth of a person by the amount of money he or she generates. So often I've seen young people with a gift and interest in teaching shift over to other jobs which neither challenged nor fulfilled them—simply because they were paid more. At the same time we have, somehow, created an atmosphere where the publisher of soft-porn magazines can become a multimillionaire and a celebrity, while a medical researcher working in an obscure laboratory seeking a cure for cancer has difficulty even supporting his family.

Most of us at one time or another flirt with the fantasy of Tevye the milk-man in the musical, *Fiddler on the Roof.* As Tevye's children marry and his world changes, he feels pressed daily with the inescapable fact of his extreme poverty. In a tender moment in the musical when he's all alone, he begins to muse on the differences money would make in his life. It's put to music and is the exciting "If I Were a Rich Man." Possibly the reason I like the song is that I've had those same fantasies myself. But when I'm at my best, I know that particular fantasy has the potential of a nightmare when making and having money becomes the driving force in our lives.

This is not a new problem. It's as old as the human race. Back in biblical times Jesus told a story about an obviously successful and prosperous farmer whose crops were so heavy that he ran out of room to store them. Faced with this dilemma, he decided it would be a good idea to tear down his barns and build bigger ones, "And there I will store all my grain and my goods. And I will say to my soul, Soul, you have ample goods laid up for many years; take your ease, eat, drink, be merry" (Luke 12:18–20). But the story ends with God saying, "Fool, this night your soul is required of you." On the surface that probably seems like harsh judgment. After all, it sounds like the farmer was just making a good business decision. But the tone of the whole story indicates that this man believed his deep needs would be met by accumulating money and material goods. I'm sure his funeral was a grand affair, and he was properly eulogized for being a sharp business man, but God's epitaph for him was "Thou fool." He wasn't a fool for dying so suddenly. His mistake was in not being satisfied with who and what he was, and in defining fulfillment in terms of what he owned.

It is easy for most of us to pass this story off by saying, "Not being satisfied is the way people are—it's just a part of being human." It is true that may be the way a lot of people feel, but, on the other hand, I know a good many people who have "got it made" and know it. And I believe that is what God intends for each of us. Some of these people are single and some are married. Among them are students, salespersons, farmers, physicians, homemakers, secretaries, lawyers, teachers—every conceivable vocation is represented. And they are just as varied in age, background, education, tastes, interests, personality, ability, social status, and visibility. But in getting to know them and in observing their lifestyle I have discovered certain general characteristics which each one seems to have in common. These characteristics define the successful life for them, and they represent one very good way of measuring our lives to see if we've got it made.

Ray and Lillian lived in a modest house in one of the older subdivisions of the city. They'd lived there since their marriage over forty years before, and while the neighborhood had changed, they seemed happy in their little home. Ray was an accountant with a small but established practice and appeared to spend more time helping some of the widows in the church with their income tax returns than he did in hunting new accounts. They had lots of friends, but never talked much about money. Consequently, I shared everyone's surprise when I read that they had given a quarter-of-a-million dollars to a Christian college to endow a chair in the business school.

But I was even more surprised as I began to hear other people's reaction to their generous gift. First, they expressed amazement that Ray and Lillian had the means to make such a generous gift. And then they'd say, "Why, with that kind of money they could have . . ." or "Lillian could have had a nicer house." Or "Ray didn't have to drive that old Chevy. He's got over a hundred thousand miles on her already." Or "They could have taken a trip around the world." It was so hard for most people to realize that a part of the secret of their life was that Ray and Lillian stayed in control of things instead of letting things control them. They had consciously rejected the idea that our worth is determined by how much we have and what we own.

I recently met a young couple who've made a similar decision about their lives. Bill and Betty have been married seven years and have two young children. Both Bill and Betty are talented and trained in their separate professions. He is an accountant, and she is a registered nurse.

Before moving to Houston they made a deliberate decision to severely limit their indebtedness. They bought a smaller house in a less expensive neighborhood even though the agent assured them that with their income they could qualify without any difficulty for a much more "substantial" and better located home.

Bill and Betty decided to spend less on automobiles and to consider them "transportation" instead of a status symbol to their peer group. Throughout their marriage they had watched the pressure of getting too deeply in debt build to a straining point among so many of their friends, and decided this was one pressure they could do without. They made a conscious decision to concentrate on the challenge of building a marriage and being good parents to their children without having to worry constantly about a budget so tight that the slightest reverse could produce a major crisis in their lives. Their values and priorities steered them clear of the vicious trap of equating quality of life with acquiring an inventory of gadgets and adult toys.

Successful People Build and Prize Human Relationships

Successful people view others not just as a part of life's scenery or as a part of the machinery that waits on them. Rather, they see others as persons of worth. My friend Glenn Carvel is single and an only child. His mother Lucille was an only child also. So when Glenn's mother died, everyone assumed he would be all alone in his grief. But they were wrong because Glenn has spent years building meaningful relationships with people. He so impressed the church with his spirit and maturity and commitment that, although he lacked the "one wife" requirement of the New Testament, he was ordained as a deacon. Glenn was also active in the music program of the church and became a part of a popular singles ensemble.

At the funeral for Glenn's mother in Westmoreland Chapel it was obvious that even though there wasn't any family to share his grief, Glenn had a host of friends who loved him and didn't intend to let him suffer the loss all alone. This illustrates an important truth. As we strive toward building a successful life, we should give careful attention to building a network of friends. And within this network, we can be strengthened and enriched by a select few who are so real and intimate that masks disappear and deep feelings can be shared without the fear of being misunderstood or judged.

There is a rash of books on how to manipulate and use people in order to get what we want. *Looking Out for Number One* and *Winning Through Intimidation* have been top sellers. But there's a hollow ring to that pagan philosophy; people who use people are painfully lonely in their success. The depression of emptiness and loneliness squeezes out any genuine sense of fulfillment. This is the type of person whom writers of detective stories always use as the victim—there are so few who grieve his passing and so many who have a legitimate reason for helping him on his way.

The importance of people seemed to come almost naturally in rural America, but in an urban society like ours today it is illusive. I recall as a boy on the farm in northeast Oklahoma what a delightful time all the young people in the community had when they went to someone's house for "Sunday Dinner." And although there were different hosts each week and varied activities, the group was always made up of the same young people. At the time, most of us were totally unaware of the invaluable influence that was at work in our lives simply by being together. Today, with our fragmented urban lifestyle, people who want to build personal relationships have to consciously work at it. It takes time and effort to establish and nourish friendships, but those who do it are richer for the investment of themselves.

I've never applied for a job or an appointment that has required me to write my life history. But if I did, I would tell my story by writing about the people who have been my friends. At almost every stage of life from my youth to the present there have been one or two significant persons who made a difference in some special way.

Beulah Morrow was such a friend. We went to the same church when I was in college. She knew me and believed in me and worried about my health when she didn't feel I was eating well or wasn't getting enough rest. During my sophomore year, our church decided to start a mission in one of the new suburbs. The task of finding and recommending a pastor was assigned to a special committee, and someone submitted my name as a likely prospect. Completely unknown to me the campus minister had made a special point of telling the committee that under no circumstance should I be considered. While he made no specific allegations, he left the impression with the committee that I wasn't the type of person they should consider. Fortunately, one member of the committee said, "Beulah Morrow knows Kenneth and can tell us if there is any substance to this criticism." Beulah came to my defense and not only discredited my critic but put in such a strong word for me that I was elected to be the first pastor of Bel Air Church. It wasn't until I resigned the church several years later that I learned of the role Beulah Morrow's friendship had played in my life at that time.

Successful People Learn To Be Comfortable with Who They Are

I remember a night years ago when Barbara and I had gone to the Summit in Houston to watch the Rockets play one of their NBA rivals. When the basketball game was over, we didn't rush for the exit like the rest of the crowd because we had to wait for our son Troy who was one of the ball boys. Standing outside the players' dressing room, I watched an interesting drama repeat itself several times. There was a little band of children collecting autographs on their programs. It was obvious that they didn't know the players well enough to identify them once they were in their street clothes. So these children were rushing up to every very tall person in the area and before they would hold their programs up to be signed one of them would ask, "Are you somebody?"

My age and height and weight made it so obvious that I was not a Houston Rocket that I never had to answer the question. As we drove home that night, I replayed the scene in my mind and wondered what I would have said if one of the children had asked, "Are you somebody?" After giving it some thought, I decided I probably would have said "no" in response to the question they were *really* asking. But then as I reflected on the question in the context of life and meaning, I knew I would have said, "Yes, I am somebody. I am me." Feeling good about ourselves keeps us from having to work so desperately to prove ourselves, and it keeps us from having to go through life auditioning for people's love and approval. Feeling good about ourselves is the foundation for emotional security. Self-esteem frees us to live life without fear.

I grew up with a healthy self-concept because of affirmation from parents, grandparents, aunts, uncles, and cousins. I was played with, talked to, and included in everything; I felt needed and wanted. But during my early teen years so many of the factors contributing to my sense of security began to crumble. Being a teenager has certain built-in anxieties, but during my adolescent years my parents divorced, our family was divided, and I had to drop out of school with a crippling case of rheumatoid arthritis. It seemed that my life was over, and I began to have grave doubts about myself. When I was at my lowest point emotionally, a group of Christian young people my age took an interest in me and began to involve me in some of their activities at the church. At the time I wasn't especially excited about church, but I was lonely and needed desperately to be with other young people. Then I began to attend church regularly, and in my moments alone I would remember some of the new and exciting things I had heard: "I was made in the image of God"; "God loves me as a person"; "Each person is gifted by God." And as the truth and power of these words filtered into my teenage mind, I gained a new sense of self-worth that has stayed with me as an adult.

Successful People Find Work Fulfilling and Worthwhile

Work, for successful people, is neither an addiction nor a drudgery but a means of self-expression and an opportunity for making a contribution to society. It is this attitude that sets them apart from people for whom work is either a compulsion they don't understand or control or a necessity to be endured but certainly not enjoyed.

I was a colleague on the seminary faculty with Dr. Wayne Oates the year he wrote the now classic book entitled *Confessions of a Workaholic.* It was a book which justifiably pointed an accusing finger at the compulsive work habits which have become so much a part of our way of life. As I worked my way through the list of characteristics of the workaholic which Dr. Oates describes so vividly, I recognized myself again and again. But I came to see that an obsession with our work and career can so easily destroy our health, our marriage, our family, and our relationship with God.

But I was a professor when that first wave of young adults for whom the "Protestant work ethic" was an obscene phrase entered graduate school. Unlike their parents, who didn't let their lives interfere with their work, these young people had no intention of letting work dominate their time. When applying for a job, they were more likely to rehearse their needs instead of expressing interest in what is expected from them in fulfilling the job. This, of course, is the other extreme. I've come to see that neither of these types have it made until they learn to relate to work in a more responsible and creative way.

Successful People Are Not Wiped Out by Failure

There is a persistent illusion that anyone who has it made can coast along without serious problems—success builds on success without any reverses. Nothing could be farther from the truth in real life. In spite of the "I've got it made" mask we wear most of the time, we all have our down periods, our low moments. We know at those times we've not measured up, and we feel disappointment and shame. To some extent we are all paralyzed by a fear of failing, and, consequently, we lose the romance of risk. And we lose the sense of adventure that comes from bold effort.

But we *will* fail, and when we do, we need to let God help us salvage good out of it and remove the fear of being destroyed by failure. In real life it is not a matter of "if we should fail" but "when we fail." And at such times, rather than waste those moments of trouble, we can, if we will, turn them over to God.

I made a discovery three years ago that has revolutionized the way I handle my troubles. I spent several months studying the life of King David, one of the significant persons in the life and religion of Israel. To me he comes closer to being a total person than anyone else in the Old Testament. I discovered that between the time he was anointed king as a boy and his actual enthronement, he spent many years as a fugitive or as an exile in the country of the Philistines.

These were years of anguish and soul-searching for David. He had his faith shaken in everyone but God: "Preserve me, O God, for in thee I take refuge" (Ps. 16:1). So strong was David's faith that he could even share his doubts: "How long, O Lord? Wilt thou forget me for ever?" (Ps. 13:1). And I'm sure there were times when in his weariness and discouragement, David wondered whether he had really been anointed as king—or whether it was just a bad dream.

My first reaction to David's fugitive years was that they seemed a sad waste of valuable time. But as I continued to study and reflect on David's life, I saw that most of the knowledge, understanding, and skills which equipped him to become king were developed not during the good times when he was in the palace, but in the difficult years when he was on the run and felt that even God had abandoned him.

During this time he established close relationships with the people of Israel and related to them in their dreams and problems. As Saul and his army pursued him, David developed skills at motivating and guiding men. It was in exile that he learned the skills of diplomacy. And it was during those fugitive experiences that he came to a deep and profound knowledge of God as he works in the ordinary day-to-day events of life.

The secret of David's life wasn't that he was trouble-free but that his troubles didn't destroy him.

Successful People Are Real Human Beings

For most of us it is intensely difficult to accept that we are finite human beings and are wrong some of the time. We strain painfully against the limitations of our humanity and insist again and again on trying to play

God. Though I am aware of the fact that it's not possible for me to know everything, there is something in my nature that makes me want to pretend I do anyway. There is the constant temptation to put on a mask and pretend to be someone I'm not.

It is at this point that God has helped me. I grew up with the general impression that there was something essentially unreal about religious people. Undoubtedly this was caused in part by the fact that most of the sermons I heard as a child were delivered in a pious-sounding, sing-song fashion replete with strange sounding jargon that left me with the impression that religious talk required a special vocabulary. That was also a time when it was considered almost heretical to admit that we had any problems after we had turned our lives over to God. As a result, the message I heard did not ring true to what I was experiencing. This caused me to doubt the validity of my experience.

It was against the backdrop of this mentality that Keith Miller wrote *The Taste of New Wine* in which he shared openly and honestly the problems he was having in trying to understand and obey God in today's complex world. This landmark book echoed the experience of thousands of people. Those who read it said, "He's a real human being." This was a freeing insight for me because my adult experience with God has taught me that he has no interest in making me look or sound like I was a visitor from some other planet. Rather, I have come to see that God will help me accept the fact that I'm a creature and not the creator. And I also believe that the acceptance of our God-given role in life makes it possible for us to become authentic human beings.

Successful People Make Commitments

One of my favorite columnists is Ellen Goodman whose three columns a week for the *Boston Globe* have been syndicated nationwide. In one of her recent articles she wrote about a friend of hers who was allergic to making commitments. When his friends chided him about this, he had a rather flip explanation. He said he viewed life as a huge buffet line where a person who made commitments could be compared to the man who filled his plate at the beginning of the line with rather ordinary fare and then after his plate was full came upon all sorts of interesting food which he liked better. With this seemingly irrefutable illustration of his position, the man let people know that all he was really doing was "keeping his options open." Ellen Goodman's evaluation was that another way of describing his action was that he was "coming to the end of the line with an empty plate."

Ellen Goodman is right in her analysis of what will happen to people who are afraid to make commitments. Actually, everything that is worthwhile in life requires the making of commitments. It is impossible for a husband and wife to build a good marriage without a commitment to each other and to the relationship. It is equally impossible to succeed in any vocation without a basic commitment to the work. Even becoming a Christian involves making a commitment of one's life to God. In fact, I am convinced that commitment is the best antidote there is for boredom and self-centeredness. It is the spice of life, and every successful person I've ever known is deeply committed in every area of his or her life.

Successful People Have Built Their Lives on a Relationship with God

I have come to see that my relationship with God is personal and not merely ritual. It is dynamic and not static; it becomes the fundamental relationship on which a meaningful life is built. It provides values by which to live and measure life, and it creates in a person a quality which allows him or her to live life to the fullest and to face death without fear.

When David was an old man and thought back on his long relationship with God, he remembered his boyhood experiences as a shepherd and portrayed the richness of his faith through the colorful phrases found in the Twenty-third Psalm. People, from small children to senior adults, find inspiration and comfort in repeating these memorable words because they describe a relationship with God that is intimate and personal, satisfying, lasting, and full of joy. David, perhaps more than anyone in the Old Testament, discovered the presence of God in every part of life, and because of this, he experienced a sense of the sacred in every circumstance.

The city in which I live is an energetic, alive, and progressive place—but it has one enormous flaw. Many of the people who live in Houston are trying to define their lives apart from a knowledge of God. But as with people everywhere across the world, my neighbors and yours can only experience genuine success through an intimate relationship with God.

Successful People Build a Support System for Their Lives and Participate in Support Systems for Others

One of the most astounding developments over the past twenty years has been our penetration into outer space. Through almost unbelievable technology NASA has successfully propelled our astronauts into space and even to the moon. This whole process has boggled my imagination, and I've been especially amazed at the complex and costly support systems that have enabled them to function in a totally alien environment. Without these support systems none of the space missions would have been successful.

What is true of the exploring of outer space applies

equally to the exploration of our inner space as we attempt to live successful lives. There was a time when I believed rather naively that the world in which I lived was friendly to all my goals and values. But the longer I live the more I'm aware of the fact that I have chosen a way which challenges many of the goals and values of our culture. While we don't need the approval of society to function, we do need a support system to help us build the kind of life that will be most fulfilling. We can survive in a city of several million if we spend a little time on a regular basis with other people who share common goals, common values, and common needs. Unlike NASA's intricate support systems, the kind we need can be built by anyone, living anywhere, and without government funding. And our support system will sustain us in all of life and then be there to help the people we love when we're gone. It's called church.

I know exactly what goes through the minds of lots of people when they read the word *church* because I was a part of that generation of Christians who specialized in telling people what was wrong with it. At the time I was doing my theological training some of the most highly respected voices in the church felt that it was "over the hill" and that some alternative needed to be worked out. I now see that all the alternatives which were suggested then won't work, and the church with all its frailties and imperfections is the primary support system for the Christian life. It helps us as we clarify our values and goals, and it gives us a different perspective from which to evaluate the world in which we live. All that we hope to become as persons under God is made more possible because of the support that is supplied in the life of the church. For the past ten years I have been part of a particular church where there is love and fellowship and sharing and ministry. I am a different person today because of this experience.

When Mike Todd, the Hollywood entrepreneur who was married to Elizabeth Taylor, was killed in a plane crash, Paul Harvey, on one of his broadcasts, commented on the untimeliness of his death. He concluded, "None of us can decide the length of our life, but we do make the decisions which determine its width and its depth." Actually, there are many things which happen in our lives over which we have no control. But we *can* decide to let God define what a successful life is for us, and we can choose to shape our lives according to his definition.

2

Getting Along with People

"DEAR ABBY, there's this boy just a year ahead of me in high school that is really cute. He says since we love each other, it is okay to make love, but I don't think it is right. Last night he told me that either we do or it's all over. I'm supposed to give him my answer when I see him next weekend. What shall I do—I don't want to lose him?"

"Dear Abby, my husband just won't sit down and talk things out with me. Then when we have a disagreement, he retreats into a shell and pouts. He just never wants to discuss anything. How can I get him to communicate with me?"

These glaring examples are the two kinds of general problems for which people most often write for advice in this type of column. The first problem and question has to do with conflicts in values. The second is related to conflicts with people—our mate, children, in-laws, boss, neighbors, or friends. But frequently the conflict with persons is closely interrelated with a conflict in values.

Both of these questions are significant for our lives. But now we will focus on the second problem—getting along with other people—and in a later chapter we will wrestle with an attempt to find a reliable means for deciding what is right and wrong. Each of us, if we are to live a successful life, must discover a valid basis for making moral and ethical decisions.

It is impossible for us to live a genuinely successful life without learning to relate to other people. Having made that somewhat dogmatic statement, I must add quickly that it is possible to pinpoint certain activities in which we can excel where getting along with others isn't of primary importance. However, this kind of success can be very shallow and short-lived.

A perfect example of this kind of shallow mentality was illustrated for me one Saturday afternoon when I was watching a professional tennis match on television. One of the contestants was John McEnroe—considered by many who were in personal contact with him to be a "self-centered brat." McEnroe had already won $250,000 that year on the circuit, and he had been a heavy favorite in this particular match, but the earlier games went against him and he had to come from behind to win the $65,000 first prize. During the course of the match McEnroe had arguments with the linesmen, the judge, and the fans, and he got so angry at his opponent that, even after winning the match, he didn't shake hands with him.

During a rehash of the match by the two television commentators, I became fascinated by their reactions to McEnroe. The first commentator was vocal in his feelings about his behavior. He then went on to praise McEnroe's skill but expressed the hope that in time he would learn how to get along with people. This comment made sense to me, but I was completely unprepared for the analysis of his partner: "I'll bet he worries about that all the way to the bank." The inference was that when you're good and are earning that much money, it doesn't make any difference how you treat people or relate to them.

As I reflected on this second statement, some rather penetrating questions came to mind: How will John McEnroe function the first time he goes to the bank to borrow money instead of putting it in? How cute will this kind of behavior be when he's no longer winning and when those same reporters are suggesting he's "over the hill"? Even while he's still at the top, what does his attitude do to those people with whom his life is inescapably tied—family, parents, coaches, tournament officials, peers, tennis fans?

Each of us is a person, and our lives are defined in relationship to persons. We do not have the option of deciding whether there will be people in our lives, but we can affect the quality of the relationship we have with them.

We can decide just how well or how poorly we will get along with people. In these relationships there is enormous potential for joy, for happiness, and for fulfillment. As I look back on some of the best times of my life, the first pictures which come to my mind are of people who knew me and cared about what happened to me. These were friends and family who loved me unconditionally. They didn't treat me like a puppet that performed acceptably only when my responses and actions conformed to their manipulations. I could be sure of their support and confidence during my low moments as well as at the peak times. The day-by-day awareness of their acceptance of me has provided courage to struggle harder in my own pilgrimage toward wholeness and personal fulfillment.

On the other hand our relationships with people have an equal potential for pain, for grief, for heartache, and for frustration. As a child of divorced parents, I was forced early in life to confront the deep hurt of ruptured relationships. And then during the past nine years, as the minister of a large urban church, I have worked and counseled with over four thousand people who had been thrust into the single world by the wreckage of their marriage. At the outset their expectations for happiness had been high, but for whatever reason their marital foundations collapsed, and next to one's own physical death there is nothing more devastating than failure in the most primary of all human relationships.

And in varying degrees the same is true of relationships with parents, children, and friends—there is always the potential of heartbreak, sorrow, and disappointment. Yet, since I believe that we can only become whole and integrated persons through relationships with others, we must come to see that we will shrivel into a dry and sterile uselessness unless we are willing to risk and invest ourselves in the lives of the people around us. Otherwise, in our self-imposed isolation, we will become desperately lonely people.

All relationships are based upon respect, and this begins with respect for ourselves as persons. Ours is a society which seems to be moving pell-mell toward total depersonalization. Consequently, it isn't easy to hold on to the idea that we are persons of worth and not just numbers in someone's impersonal computer. In fact, I think most people today share the common feeling that their personhood has been sacrificed on an altar made of plastic cards and numbers.

When I was a child one of my favorite radio programs was the classic "Fibber McGee and Molly." One of the routines which appeared in every show occurred when Fibber picked up the phone to call someone. He began by saying, "Operator, connect me with Jackson 4127." And after a momentary pause, he would ask the operator, "Is that you, Myrt?" It always was, and they would visit a minute about the latest gossip and what was happening around town.

What a vivid contrast with today's telephone calls! Of course, it is faster and less expensive to dial the area code and number I want, but I do miss a helpful sounding human voice. That seems, though, to be pretty much a part of the past except when I'm making a call and charging it to my telephone credit card. Then the operator comes on the line and asks for my card number. I rather like the friendly sound of her voice, but now and then I'm jolted back to the present when the operator asks, "Will you give me your number again, please? The computer didn't take it." Immediately, I feel let down because here is a fresh reminder that I'm dependent on an impersonal computer, and I resent it. Each of us are persons—flesh and blood human beings—and our emotional, spiritual, and physical health requires positive interchange that comes through relationships with other people.

Learning the art of getting along with people is a lifetime effort. In fact, even with all of our striving we'll never perfect that art, but continued, conscious effort will improve our skills. Of one thing I'm sure, it won't happen by listening to cassette tapes, reading a book on the subject, or listening to a lecture, as helpful as these may be. Rather, it is learned by experience as we live out our lives. Our ability to get along with other people is dependent upon the attitudes we have toward life—our appreciation for the worth of others and ourselves. It is related to our growing understanding of human nature and human behavior and how well we learn from our mistakes and from others. Above all, though, the scope and range of our relationships is determined to a large degree by how well we have consciously and unconsciously funneled all that we have learned and experienced into the practical, day-to-day task of getting along with people.

But as in every other part of life, we need goals and standards if we are to grow and mature into attractive and productive persons. Establishing standards and goals will give us a basis for evaluating how we treat people and how we are being treated. None of the following suggestions are unique or original; they are simply efforts to implement the command to "do unto others as you would have others to do unto you," and in the process our awareness level may be raised.

People Are More Than Their Function

It is a natural and unfortunate tendency for people to get their identity totally from their work. As a result you may ask someone, "Who are you?" and instead of giving their name, they will identify themselves by what they do. This is one reason why so many retired persons lose interest in life—they have no present frame of reference. I've come to feel there's nothing more destructive to any relationship than viewing another person in terms of what they do to earn a living. Stereotypes are dreadfully impersonal.

My father was never good at remembering names, but he had a marvelous memory for associating interests or activities with a person. He lived for a time before his death on the Arroyo Hondo in the Rio Grande Valley of Texas. I remember visiting with him as he sat on his dock at night fishing for trout, and he would tell me about his neighbors. He would point to a particular house and then explain who they were in terms of what they do. I can still recall his pointing to the third house down the street and saying, "That's where the alligator gar man lives." I knew exactly what he meant. He was the man who spent each day in his little boat catching giant alligator gar which he marketed in Rio Hondo. Though I didn't say anything to him at the time, I felt that his description tended to belittle the man.

After that experience I watched myself as I came in contact with people, and I realized that I had fallen into the same trap—except the names were different. There was the "waitress at the restaurant," the "teller at the bank," the "man at the service station," and the "pharmacist at the drugstore." In my hurry to be waited on I had reduced them in my mind to the function which they performed for me. I had to remind myself that each of them was a person with a name, family, feelings, interests, talents, plans, and needs. While it is true that we do not have time to become involved in a deep personal relationship with all the people we meet, we can at least remember that they are persons, too.

Develop the Art of Listening

One of the best tools in developing relationships with people is the ear. Several years ago the prolific and insightful writer Dr. John Drakeford wrote a book entitled *The Awesome Power of the Listening Ear.* John and I have been friends for years, and one time when we were together in Fort Worth where he teaches, we were discussing the counseling center he had established. He told me that it was doing well and in giving the reason for its success he added, "You know, Kenneth, that we have highly qualified counselors in the center, but one of the main reasons for our success is that most of the people who come to us desperately need someone to really listen to them. And that is precisely what we try to do."

As I think about the people whose friendships have made an impact on my life, I remember the times they not only shared ideas and themselves with me, but they listened to me with interest and concern. From time to time I've seen teenagers gravitate into what seemed to be a most unlikely relationship with a certain adult. Then later I would learn that the bond was created by the person's interest in them and that he or she listened as the teenager played aloud the ideas, the decisions, and the frustrations of his or her life. There is healing in listening, as any married couple knows who takes time at the end of the day to focus attention on each other to the exclusion of all other distractions. And parents who take time and care enough to really listen to their children are making a rich investment in the health of their family and in the future of each member.

Listening Involves Eyes as Well as Ears

The act of listening authentically to the people around us calls for the use of our eyes as well as our ears. All of us have a way of unconsciously communicating with our whole being, and this "body language" must be listened to also. A friend of mine who is an expert in the whole field of human communication once said to me, "Kenneth, most people are not verbal. They have a difficult time putting into words the things which bother them. Consequently, people who deal with people need to learn to watch for all sorts of non-verbal communication such as the facial expression, the tone of voice, the posture, or the eye-contact or lack of it. Often the body communicates the opposite of what the person is saying. Believe the body."

At first I discounted his conclusion. But as I thought about and became more aware of what to look for, it began to make a lot of sense. So often, I realized, the first signals of a cry for help didn't flash from what was said but from the way a person looked or acted.

I had never met Carol before she arrived at my office

for her appointment. She seemed a bit nervous and apparently found it difficult to either sit still or look directly at me. Since she didn't seem to know how to start the conversation, I asked, "Carol, tell me what I can do for you." Her response was a rather noncommittal, "Oh nothing. You know my father because I think the two of you were in seminary together. Well, I was talking to him on the phone Sunday, and he suggested that I ought to drop in on you sometime and bring his greetings."

Obviously, Carol knew that wasn't her real reason for being in my office, and from her body language, I was equally sure that her words were just a mask behind which the real motive was hiding. After I had asked two or three gentle questions and had listened attentively to her responses, Carol began to relax and found the words to tell me where and why she was hurting. She described her feelings of concern for her eight-year-old daughter who suffered from a severe learning disability. As a top administrator in the company where she worked, the demands on Carol's time and emotions were enormous. Feelings of guilt and stress had her on an emotional seesaw as she struggled to meet her own needs and those of her handicapped daughter. All of this would have been lost, however, if I had accepted Carol's opening innocuous comment and had failed to pick up her other signals of distress.

Listening Involves the Heart

The sensitive and caring listener is often tuned in to the deeper levels of life and can recognize a larger but unexpressed need. This was true in the story of four men who tried to take their crippled friend to Jesus. But the house where Jesus was teaching was so jammed with people that they couldn't get close to him at all. So, in their determination they tore a hole in the roof and lowered their friend down on a stretcher right in front of Jesus.

The boldness of this interruption was surely felt by the whole crowd, as Jesus stopped talking and looked intensely at the man lying at his feet. The story tells us that Jesus was moved with compassion at the man's physical disability, but he saw beyond that and sensed a deeper need. With his penetrating insight, Jesus saw and understood this man's deep need—possibly never felt or expressed before—for the healing forgiveness of God that would free him from the guilt of sin. And in response to this, Jesus' first words to the cripple were, "Thy sins are forgiven." Imagine the amazement of that crowd! But then their credulity was further strained when Jesus spoke the words that healed his body.

Since his father's death Jim's mother had been living with him. But a fall and lengthy hospitalization convinced Jim and his family that they could no longer care for his mother, so she was placed in a nearby rest home. In my conversations with Jim I began to see that he was very concerned about his mother and her reactions to the rest home. Almost every time we were together he would say, "I hope you'll continue to remember mom in your prayers. She's having a hard time adjusting." One day, after one of our visits, it suddenly dawned on me that while I had been *hearing* Jim, I hadn't really been listening.

As I pondered this new thought and reflected on Jim's problems, it suddenly occurred to me that his greatest need was for himself and not for his mother. So I sat down at my desk and wrote Jim a note telling him how fortunate I felt his mother was to have a son who cared as much for her as he did. I reassured him that I believed he had made the wisest and most loving decision possible when he put her in the rest home. Later he said to me, "You'll never know how freeing it was for me to get your note. I hadn't really admitted to myself that I was letting a feeling of guilt wipe me out."

One of my favorite public speakers is Millie Dienert of Philadelphia, Pennsylvania. Recently I heard Millie speak to several hundred ministers and their spouses on "Redeeming the Time" (taken from the phrase in the Apostle Paul's writing). Frankly, I wasn't particularly turned on when she announced her subject because almost everyone I'd ever heard speak on that theme had given a ringing call to frantic activity. But Millie captured my attention in the introduction when she insisted that all of us are too busy and need to re-order our priorities and take time for more important things than those which presently fill our schedule. And one of those more important things was "We need to make more time to listen." Then she told about what happened at her minister father's funeral. As people expressed sympathy and spoke appreciatively of her father, no one mentioned his sermons, or the church he had built, or the organizations he had started. Most everyone that spoke to her expressed some variation of this comment, "He had time for me. He always listened to me, and he cared."

Avoid Treating People Like Objects

Peter seemed to have more friends than most people. I seldom heard him criticized, and this was particularly noticeable because his work placed him in contact with people under circumstances which frequently created differences of opinions. While visiting with a friend of Peter's who had also worked for him at one time, I asked, "What's his secret for getting along so well with people?" She smiled and confessed, "I wondered about that when I first started working for him. I was surprised that a person as demanding and direct as he is could be so well liked. But I didn't really figure it out until I asked myself why I like him, and that's when I learned his secret: Peter always treated me like a person and not a thing. No matter what he asked me to do, I never had the feeling that he had forgotten about me as a person." The existential philosophers in their distinction between "I-it" and "I-thou" relationships remind us that a person is a "thou" and not an object or a thing.

A classic example of reducing people to objects is found in magazines of the *Playboy* genre. Whether you are reading the ads, the articles, or looking at the pictures the message is the same: women are sex objects and not persons. Their role is to titillate and cater to a male population that is inwardly frightened of responsible relationships with women as persons. Their false gospel says that sex is just another appetite to be satisfied without concern for relationships or commitments. Unfortunately, the huge circulation of magazines of this type attract many well-known writers, but the results are an ill-concealed downgrading of women as persons.

But the temptation to treat people as objects has infiltrated almost every segment of our society, even those areas that usually are more interested in people. I have a friend who is a very good surgeon. He feels that his profession as a doctor is just as much a ministry for God as it would be if he were the pastor of a church. As a young man my friend did a residency in a specialized surgery in one of the great teaching hospitals in this country. His dedication and skills so impressed those in charge that he was offered a coveted position on the staff. But to their great surprise he turned it down.

His main reason for rejecting the offer was that he felt the hospital staff was more interested in the disease than in the people they treated. For example, he said, "I examined an elderly man who had a very bad facial cancer. After consulting with my colleagues, it was agreed that there was nothing we could do either to save his life or prolong it. So, I had a conference with the patient and told him that I could do surgery, but it would not really help. I advised him to check out of the hospital, go home, make peace with God, set his house in order, and die with dignity. When my supervisor heard what I told the patient, he reprimanded me by saying, 'You should never do that. A chance to cut is a chance to learn.' He may be right, but to me the patient is still a person whom God loves, and I need to treat him or her that way."

Successful People Look Beyond the Stereotypes

One of the greatest barriers to getting along with others is the number of stereotypes which distort our understanding of people and inhibit our communication with them. Stereotypes tend to be oversimplified, generalized, inadequate, and misleading labels which we attach to persons, and they function as roadblocks to healthy relationships.

Many people tend to think that the only stereotypes are racial. And it's true that there are a seemingly endless number of these. I recall a locked-in, older friend of mine who actually thought that "all blacks played the banjo." Over the years I introduced him to a number of distinguished black ministers, most of whom had almost no special musical talent. But he clung tenaciously to this distorted picture.

There are many other ways in which we are crippled in our relationships because of stereotypes. For example, there is the vocational stereotype. While I was a professor in graduate school, I tried to show my students how their attitudes toward a person's job could affect their relationships. Almost all of them planned to become ministers and shared the feeling that they "loved everybody." To get beyond that little bit of self-deception, I began the class one day with a word-association game. I had a list of ten words. As I called out each word the students were supposed to write down the first thing that came to mind. One of the words was *waitress.*

When the class members began to share their first impressions of a waitress, it was obvious that what they had was a string of unkind caricatures and not really a picture of a person. The list included *dumb, flirt, immoral, uneducated,* and *failure.* They had fallen into the trap of defining the *person* in terms of a caricature.

I know what it's like to be the object of stereotype thinking. Shortly after arriving in Houston, I was invited to address Downtown Rotary, the largest Rotary Club in the world. It met in the ballroom of the famous old Houston landmark, the Rice Hotel. The ballroom was on the mezzanine floor, so when I entered the lobby, I made my way to the large escalator. Everyone on the escalator was going to the same meeting so there was a good amount of friendly visiting. The man next to me nodded and asked, "Are you a member of this club?" When I told him that I was just there as a visitor, he said, apologetically, "You sure picked a heck of a day to visit. We've got some preacher speaking." I didn't bother to tell him that I was the speaker. But I was reminded once again how many people who don't even know me have decided what I'm like because of their stereotype of a minister.

Then there are all sorts of social stereotypes. When Vance Packard's book *The Status Seekers* became a best seller, one of my friends read it and decided that he had found the golden key for really understanding people. One day in his great enthusiasm he said to me, "When I find out the kind of car a person drives, where he buys his clothes, where he went to college, and what books he read last year, I can tell you *all* about him." Packard's book was just one of the first of an endless stream of writing that attempts to clue us in to what's "in" and what's "out." All of these are lazy and superficial ways of deciding about people.

All of the notoriety given the women's movement the past several years has pointed out a number of sexual stereotypes we have had about both men and women. When I was a teenager, I worked at a soda fountain/grill. It was a two-person operation, and both of us worked the fountain, sandwich board, grill, and steam table. And we washed the dishes when there was a lull in business. So when Barbara and I married I not only knew my way around the kitchen, but I had also learned to enjoy cooking. One day a couple of our friends dropped in for lunch, and because Barbara and I were on a tight time schedule, I went into the kitchen to help. My friend was scandalized. "Men don't cook," he said with shock and disapproval. "This one does," I replied. Unfortunately, there are a lot of conclusions we've come to about males and females which have nothing to do with ability or interest but reflect a culturally-conditioned idea which needs to be re-examined.

Our daughter Nancy is in her third year of study at the University of Michigan Law School. Between her first and second years she worked as a law clerk for a small progressive firm in Houston. One day she came home with glowing reports of the way the partners accepted the fact that she was a woman law clerk. But what she hadn't counted on was the attitudes of most of the clients. When she and one of the male clerks were both involved in meetings with a client, Nancy was usually asked to "take notes of the meeting" because it was just assumed that she was a secretary.

Living in a world of stereotypes not only seriously distorts our relationships with other people, but I believe it causes us to become stunted in our own development.

People who play the stereotype game just aren't pleasant to be around.

Successful People Learn To Be Open and Honest

The truly successful people I know have learned to be open and honest about their feelings. However, this doesn't mean that we can be brutally frank with everyone and blurt out whatever comes to mind in the name of being "open." This can be a cruel and destructive practice. There are times that relating to people means we will respond to the emotion behind the question and not to the literal question. For example, when a wife says to her husband with tears in her eyes, "Do you think I'm too fat?" she isn't really interested in his reaction to her weight. But she is asking for assurance that her husband loves her even though she has gained weight. At times like this a wise husband will ignore the words in the question and respond to the meaning behind those words.

I learned early in life that I sometimes ask questions I really don't want answered. One day after a meeting of the student council at school, my girl friend Mary Lou and I were walking home together. I was feeling pretty good about myself, but I was after a little affirmation from Mary Lou, so I said, "You and I are good friends, and you know me well. I know I'm not perfect. What do you think are my weak points. Be brutally frank." Actually, I didn't think I had any, but I was just fishing for a compliment. I discovered that, even though we were good friends, she was keeping a list on me. My question gave her a chance to be "open," so she really unloaded on me. Mary Lou hadn't heard my real question—her "honesty" was a crushing blow to my feelings.

There is a kind of honesty and openness that should be possible in the day-to-day routines of life that does not threaten and endanger relationships. So many times I've watched people go along with some proposal in a committee without saying a word, and then later during a coffee break say, "That's the dumbest thing we've ever done." When I've asked them why they didn't speak up during the meeting, they often say, "I don't like to make waves. People who raise questions just don't get ahead around here." This is probably the number one reason why so much of the planning within the structures of large organizations doesn't seem to have been thought through. Most of the people involved didn't contribute because they were afraid of creating tension and were more anxious to please than to make a contribution. Any situation where we "feel" at one level and "participate" at another is unhealthy.

It is true there is more risk involved in being open and honest, but there are enough advantages to make it worthwhile: we are more apt to make a contribution; we'll learn more in honest dialogue than in sullen approval; we will find it easier to work on a project that has some of our ideas in it.

When we express our feelings and opinions in an open but tactful way, people who really matter will have more respect for us, and we will like ourselves better.

Successful People Learn How To Start Over with Others

The one thing we can be sure of in relating to people is that things will go badly at times. It is ridiculous to think that others will always understand us or that we will see things their way. Tense moments are part of every relationship. A sensitive and caring person is aware of this, and knows that at such times it is important to find a way to start over with people after a bad experience.

The key to starting over with people is wrapped up

in one little eleven-letter word—*forgiveness.* Unfortunately, we often think of forgiveness as a sign of weakness, of a softness when it comes to "who's right" and "who's wrong" in a disagreement or difference of opinion. There's always danger of feeling we will lose face if we work things out with someone who has "done us wrong." This is the kind of distorted thinking which leads to long-term grudges and to crippling bitterness and resentment.

Forgiveness isn't pretending nothing has happened, or pretending that what happened didn't hurt. It isn't even forgetting it completely, and it isn't going back and starting over as though it hadn't ever happened. Instead, forgiveness is refusing to let anything permanently destroy the relationship. There's a place for saying, "I'm sorry." There's a place for assuring the other person that "all is forgiven." But the goal of both is to rebuild the relationship. One of the amazing things about a healthy beginning again is that the relationship is often stronger than it was before.

This was a problem Jesus' disciples wrestled with years ago. In a conversation one day, they were trying to decide just how many times they should forgive someone and start over. For a long time that seemed like a silly question to me, but the experiences of living and relating to people have made me painfully aware that both forgiving and being forgiven are costly. There is pain in admitting the responsibility for the things we have done wrong, and often it is easier to say the words of forgiveness than it is to mean them with our hearts. God sometimes has to help me see when I am wrong and then give me the courage to admit it. But where I really need help is in being willing to start over with people who have either hurt me or someone I love. The fact that God continues to forgive me gives me a model, but it doesn't solve all my feelings. This is why a part of my prayer as I begin each day is "Help me to love the people I come in contact with the way you do." I know that learning how to forgive will enhance my ability to get along with people.

The Model for Relating to People

Successful people will find help in relating to others from a better understanding of how God relates to us.

For years the idea of loving people as God loves them was nothing more to me than a lovely abstraction. Then I was asked to prepare a new elective course on "The Soulwinning Interviews of Jesus." Since I taught in the Department of Evangelism at a seminary, I'm sure I was expected to discover and map out Jesus' evangelistic technique. I began my preparations with the reading and studying of all the conversations which Jesus had with other people as they are told in the Gospels. Again and again I saw that his love allowed him to cross the social, racial, and religious barriers of his time. Jesus conversed with a wide range of people and seemed comfortable with them. He was not exclusive in his relationships, and he didn't mix only with people who thought like he did. In fact, he was secure enough to be seen with people who were apparent failures and misfits without fearing for his reputation. He was honest with his friends when it upset them, and with his enemies when it got him into trouble. His capacity to love people was the key.

It's easy to discover the rhetoric of "God's love," but it is much harder to translate what that love means in all the many relationships of life. Consequently, many people learn the words and never experience the reality. I know a man who in his relationships with others always insists on his own way, but he thinks of himself as a very spiritual human being because after he's run over someone he always smiles and says, "I love you."

Obviously we'll not be able to measure up completely to the model Jesus has given us. But as we are able to see and care for people a little more from his perspective, we will find it easier to love them the way he does. And it is out of a genuine caring and concern for others that we slowly, and at times painfully, begin to learn the art of getting along with people.

3

Discovering You're Needed

UNLIKE SOME OF John Steinbeck's novels, *Travels with Charley* is an easy-reading philosophical travelogue. It is the delightful and intriguing story of Steinbeck's travels across America in a self-contained camper with only his dog, Charley, for company.

During his earlier years, John Steinbeck had established himself as a top-selling, Pulitzer prize-winning author. He wove into story form the complex passions felt and lived by the flood of migrants that poured into the Central Valley of California during the Great Depression of the 1930s. His *Of Mice and Men* and *Grapes of Wrath* laid bare the agonies and joys and frustrations of a subculture unique to those days.

But as the years passed, Steinbeck began to suspect that he had lost touch with the pulse of America. So he set out with Charley to rediscover the land and the people whose vigor and strength made us great. From New York City they wound their way westward to the shores of the Pacific Northwest, down the coast of California, east across the desert states, and full circle from the South back to Manhattan. Steinbeck traveled incognito; he and Charley had no set plan.

Everywhere they stopped, whether to camp for a week in some pleasant place or to have lunch in a desert truck stop, he talked with people and listened to them. Steinbeck carefully recorded his impressions, hoping that a picture of the "real American" would emerge.

One of the most profound statements in the book was the reaction most people had to Steinbeck's gypsy life-style. He said that everywhere he went people would say, "I'd like to climb in the truck and go with you." Even when Steinbeck reminded them that they didn't even know where he was going, they still insisted they'd like to go. In response to his question as to whether they were unhappy where they were, they would reply invariably, "No, but I'd still like to take off with you."

After this experience repeated itself again and again in every part of the country and with many different types of people, Steinbeck came to the rather sad conclusion that "nearly everyone in this country wishes he were someone else, living somewhere else, doing something else." I believe this comment describes a kind of restlessness that pervades our society today—a restlessness that robs us of a sense of satisfaction and fulfillment.

While I'm inclined to agree in general with Steinbeck's observation, I'm happy to report that I know a good many people for whom just the opposite is true. An awareness of this truth sent me on a search for the difference between the restless and dissatisfied people and the contented and fulfilled people. This is what I've discovered: the satisfied people believe they have specific talent and ability and have made a conscious effort to develop those gifts and through them are making a creative contribution to society. They have a sense of satisfaction that grows out of being needed. We seem to be able to handle not being liked by everyone or not being rich or not being healthy all the time, but the most tragic emotion that can tear at our insides is the feeling of not being needed. This breeds more unhappiness with people of all ages and conditions than anything I know.

During the many years I've spoken to conventions, taught in seminaries, served as a pastor in churches, and talked with people wherever I could, I have also listened to people as they shared painful feelings of discouragement. But in most instances they were at the time unaware of the underlying cause. More often than not, however, the tone of each conversation revealed that their feelings of discouragement and inadequacy grew out of the fact that they had not discovered and accepted and developed their talents and gifts. They were living in sort of a vacuum—without a deep sense of purpose or of feeling needed.

It's not always easy to find a situation and a lifestyle in which we feel necessary. Sometimes the conditions and environment must be right before we find our niche and start to grow.

When I moved to Fort Worth, Texas, in the fall of 1952, the area was in the midst of one of the worst droughts in years. The fields surrounding the city and stretching out across North Texas were a burned-out brown, and the raw earth was criss-crossed with deep cracks. Since this was my introduction to this part of North Texas, I just assumed it was always that way, and I came to accept all of this as normal. However, a year or so later, there were drought-breaking rains. A lake formed behind the Corps of Engineers Dam at Benbrook, the Trinity River began to flow again, and the trees and fields began to show green. But my greatest surprise came as I drove out from town in the springtime to discover acres and acres of bluebonnets where before there had been only withered and dried grass. When I mentioned my amazement to one of the long-time residents, he explained, "Those bluebonnet seeds have been lying there in the soil for seven years waiting for the conditions to be right for them to germinate and come up." As I reflected on this marvelous provision of God through the wonders of nature, the thought occurred to me that this was descriptive of most of us. For whatever reason, our talents and abilities remain dormant and useless—waiting for just the right conditions. I've also come to feel that there are certain steps we can take which will help create those conditions.

As I was growing up in the rural, earthy conditions characteristic of Oklahoma farm life, I developed, even then, a passion for discovering my talents and abilities because of my desire to exceed and be accepted, but I had little guidance or help. In high school I took all those tests which were supposed to reveal my real aptitudes. And through the years I've read books, attended special lectures, and enrolled in seminars designed to give me a better understanding of what I could do with my life. I'm sure all of this made some contribution to my search, but I was in the middle of my career as a minister before I discovered a whole series of insights which gave me a handle on how we need to feel and think about our own special talents and abilities. But the interesting thing is that I made my new discovery by thinking through and coming to an understanding for the first time of a little story that I read as a child.

Jesus had a habit of taking a very profound concept and illustrating it with a story right out of everyday life. While sitting on a hillside with his disciples one day, he told the story of a very wealthy man who was planning to take a long trip far away from his home. He decided that while he was gone he would trust some of his capital to three of his employees. He knew the men well, so he gave them amounts of money which were commensurate with their abilities. Two of the men invested their share of the money carefully, but the man who was given the smallest amount was frightened by the responsibility. So rather than take the risk of investing the capital, he hid it where it would be safe and couldn't be stolen.

When the owner finally returned and called for an accounting, the first two men explained that they had doubled their amount through a wise investment. Even though the amounts were different his response was the same to both men, "Well done . . . you have been faithful over a little, I will set you over much" (Matt. 25:23). The unimaginative and fearful man who had just hid his share of the money in a safe place returned the exact amount he had been given with the explanation that because he felt the owner was a hard and unreasonable man, he had been afraid to take any risk. So, according to the story, the owner took the money away from him and gave it to the men who had the most. Then he fired the man on the spot and had him thrown out.

The key idea of this story is that we can be happy and fulfilled if we are able to *accept* the gifts and talents we have, *develop* them to the degree possible, and *dedicate* them to God and to others. And in doing this we are then able to move forward with confidence toward a successful life; we are on the way toward finding an expanded sense of meaning, a new identity, an enlarged purpose, and a fresh warmth and intimacy in our relationship with others.

Successful People Accept Their Gifts and Talents

I have been surprised to discover that more people seem to have difficulty accepting their gifts and abilities than they do in either developing or dedicating them. It is possible that most of us have devoted our energies to the idea that a person should not "think of himself more highly than he ought to think" (Rom. 12:3) to the exclusion of a balancing awareness of the danger of putting too low an estimate on our ability and gifts. Unfortunately, many people today suffer from such a low self-esteem that they're convinced they don't have any talent worth developing.

One day I was going through a stack of new books I had just received from my publisher. There wasn't time to read all of them carefully so I was just scanning them. In the middle of the stack I came upon a book which had a blank page about a third of the way through. While I was trying to figure out what had happened, one of my students tapped on the door and asked if I had a minute to talk with him. Before he could get settled down, I told him about my book with the blank page. "Can you believe that," I said, "Page sixty-seven is blank. Pages sixty-six and sixty-eight are printed, but where sixty-seven should be, the page is blank."

I don't think I really expected any response from the student, but he became very quiet, and then said in all seriousness, "I think I know just how page sixty-seven feels."

This young man was from a family of talented parents who were achievers; his brothers and sisters had outstanding ability. But when he compared himself to his family and friends, he had come to question whether or not he really had anything worth contributing to life. In comparing his life to a book, he felt like a blank surrounded by interesting and exciting pages—and he could identify personally with that snafu in the printing plant. We talked on for quite a while, and I tried to help him begin to feel good about himself, to become convinced that he could be a successful person. At the time, though, I believed it was quite unusual for a young person to feel that way about himself. Somehow I hadn't realized just how common this attitude is today.

Several months later I went to Laity Lodge in the Hill Country of Southwest Texas to be one of the leaders for a couples retreat. Keith Miller had only recently become a Christian, but he had been asked by Howard Butt to direct the program. This was even before Keith had written the now classic book, *The Taste of New Wine,* and was at the time that the first rumblings of spiritual renewal within the laity of the church were being heard.

In one of my talks I shared my experience with the student who identified himself with the blank page in the book. It was almost an aside remark, so I really didn't expect any response. But to my surprise during the rest of the retreat I had more than a dozen people say to me, "I'm like that boy who came to your office."

Every one of the people who said that to me seemed attractive, intelligent, and talented. Outwardly they looked successful . . . as if they had it made. But down deep inside they felt unsure, insecure—blank pages. A long time ago a wise man was inspired to write to people just like us, "There are varieties of gifts, but the same Spirit; and there are varieties of service, but the same Lord; and there are varieties of working, but it is the same God who inspires them all in every one. To each is given the manifestation of the Spirit for the common good" (1 Cor. 12:4–7).

When we think about the uniqueness of our lives, it is sometimes difficult to translate this very profound truth into the categories we work with today. The writer who has helped me most with these concepts is Elizabeth O'Connor in her small but powerful book, *The Eighth Day of Creation.* She writes about persons discovering and claiming gifts, and she stresses the role other people can have in this process. When the book was published,

I read and underlined it and felt challenged by much of what she said. This occurred at a time when I was working with a growing restlessness in a position where I felt most of my best gifts were unused and much of my life was being spent with details in which I had less talent and virtually no interest. But even though the message of the book haunted me, I laid it aside and threw myself with renewed energy into my job.

A couple of years later when I was approached by the committee from the church which brought me to Houston, I went back and re-read my underlines, and they leaped off those pages like bolts of lightning. This time I read through a new set of lenses. I saw that if I continued to play at functioning in a position which left unused some of the finest of my gifts, then something in me that was very precious would die. I was energized by that new feeling—yet if it had not been for the encouragement of a handful of people who knew me and encouraged me, I still might not have made the move which affirmed my own gifts and my greatest usefulness.

I believe the basic insight for feeling good about our talents and gifts is a religious one. Deep within us there is the awareness of being the creation of a purposeful God, and it is from this source that we can receive an assurance of meaning and worth. My niece is a very talented wildlife artist. Although much of her painting focuses on frogs and turtles and crayfish, her interest takes in all of life. More than anyone else Carol helped me to understand the "ecological chain" which ties all of life together and gives it purpose. One day while she was visiting our farm, we were sitting in the back yard when she noticed that a large brown bird had built its nest on the lowest limb of a small walnut tree just outside the fence. "That's a cuckoo bird. It's very important to you because it feeds on the bagworms which infest the pecan trees in this area." She is a firm believer in the idea that if something exists, it has a purpose and is important. Unfortunately, so often, we somehow discover the usefulness of lesser creatures and things before we find our own.

There is a much stronger foundation, though, for affirming our gifts and talents in the call to discipleship. When God invites a person into a personal relationship with him (as he does all), it is an invitation to realize one's own significance.

In thinking back to the story Jesus told about the man who hid his talent, I've come to see that the man's biggest problem was the warped picture he had of the owner. It filled him with fear and kept him from investing the money wisely. Instead of accounting for his own action, he attacked the owner for being a hard man whose wealth came too much from the work of others. While I know that there are many gifted people who never acknowledge God as the source for their talents, I believe he is the source of help for us in the accepting and perfecting of our gifts and talents. When the "giver" is acknowledged it becomes easier to use the gifts for the good of others, and it's easier to resist the temptation to use them in a self-centered way. The talents which are used to fuel ego trips often become self-destructive. On the other hand, talents which are spent on others have healing in them for everyone.

A truly great liberating experience comes when we are able to accept our gifts as unique, valuable, and needed. This frees us from imitation and from feeling the need to compete with everyone. It frees us from feelings of envy and releases us to appreciate people. It makes us know that we have something to contribute to life and that we are needed. Unfortunately, there are those in every group who seem to feel the need to "put down" everybody else. This "put down" attitude usually signals that the guilty person does not feel good about himself. He lives with the mistaken notion that lowering everyone else a notch will make him feel taller. But, on the other hand when we are around a person who both sees and celebrates the uniqueness in others, we can be quite sure that he or she has a healthy sense of self-esteem.

Our Talents Must Be Developed

I recall the first confrontation I ever had with a person who thought that bright, creative people didn't need to develop practical skills. It occurred shortly after Dan Yeary resigned as minister to single adults at our church. Dan was an exceptionally effective and well-organized leader. And as a result of his outstanding work, our church had been given *Guidepost* magazine's "Church of the Year Award." It was terribly important to us to replace Dan with someone of his caliber.

Less than a week after Dan's intention to leave had been publicized, I received a telephone call from a person who was interested in the position. He began by saying, "I understand that Yeary was a very talented and creative man," and I assured him that this was accurate. He then shared with me, with appropriate modesty, that he was considered to be both talented and creative and would be willing to talk with me about the position.

I told him that I had not even had time to re-think the job description or make a list of possible persons, but that I would be happy to talk with him. So, we continued our conversation, but since I didn't know him, I decided to bypass at this time certain of the obvious questions and get right down to specifics: "How are you at enlisting and training and supervising adults in a Bible study ministry program?" After a short pause he said that wasn't his "thing."

Frankly, I was a bit taken back by this response, but I went on to the second question, "Do you have any training and experience either in group processes or one-to-one counseling?" His reply to this was that he "wasn't *into* the counseling *thing*."

I decided to give it one more try, and since one of the major parts of the job would be designing and managing seminars for singles, I asked if he had either experience or interest in this kind of ministry and was told, "Quite frankly that sort of thing doesn't turn me on."

When I finally asked him what kind of job he wanted, he replied without any embarrassment, "One that needs a person who is talented and creative." It appeared quite obvious to me that he seemed to be living with the illusion that being creative was a substitute for the bone-grinding work involved in developing and sharpening our talents.

I had an experience during my senior year in college—which has become sort of a parable to me—of the temptation each of us has to not really develop our talents to the fullest extent. As an education student at the University of New Mexico, I was required to be a practice teacher in the high school during my last semester. My major was English Literature so I was assigned one of the three junior level Modern Literature classes. At that particular time Albuquerque High School divided each class into three sections by I.Q. ratings. The sections were made up into "X," "Y," and "Z" groups with the naïve assumption that no one would suspect the meaning of the classification. It soon became clear, though, that everyone assumed those in the "X" group were above average, those in the "Y" group were average, and anyone in the "Z" group was borderline at best. I was assigned to teach the "Z" group, and my classmates suggested that my professors had matched me with the appropriate class.

During the semester I came to know each of the young people in the class very well, and I soon discovered an interesting pattern in their behavior. On a test which determined the grade they would get in the class, they all worked hard and did well. However, on any test which they suspected had any possibility of reclassifying them either "X" or "Y," they left every other question blank. To my knowledge there were only one or two persons in the entire class who were limited in their talent and ability. The rest had decided to get by with the least possible effort. The sad thing about it was that they were sabotaging their own potential for success by their laziness.

I once listened to Billy Graham do a question-and-answer session at a theological seminary with a group of young ministerial students. One young man, obviously tired of Greek and Hebrew and classes in theology and eager to get out into the work, asked, "Dr. Graham, if you were my age with the world in the shape it's in, would you still spend several years just in training?"

I think Dr. Graham's answer surprised everyone, "Young man, I cannot think of a better use for your time right now than developing the gifts God has given you. If you were told to go into the woods to cut down trees and were given an ax which was made of good steel but was dull, the time spent sharpening the ax would not be considered wasted. Stay in school and sharpen your ax."

Good advice, but not always easy to follow. It is important that we understand and accept the fact that it may take years for our talents and gifts to assume their potential. We knew by what our son Troy did with his first set of Lego blocks that he had a talent for design. Without our guidance, he was putting together combinations that were out of the ordinary. Now, years later, he has completed his first year of university study in mechanical engineering. Between the first interest and the present there has been lots of work and development—and a tremendous amount of work and effort will be required to take him from this point to where he will be a practicing engineer. But that is what life is all about—developing our gifts and talents. This is the pattern for all of us irrespective of our particular gift or talent. The person who is working at developing his talent is never wasting time. For it is in the perfecting of our abilities and their use for creative purposes that we come to discover we are needed and worthwhile.

Successful People Separate Talents and Vocation

It is very natural for us to equate our talent and our job. While it is important for our regular employment to reflect our gifts and interests, there is no way one job can ever be an outlet for all our capabilities. Unfortunately, many young adults complete their training and enter into the job market with a very idealized picture of what their vocation is going to do for them. Somehow they have come to believe that it will be the outlet for all their ideas, interests, and energy. But they soon find that isn't true and become restless. Instead of deciding to supplement their primary job with different ways of expressing their uniqueness, they decide they are in the wrong place and start to hop around. There is still the feeling, which many of us share to some degree, that somewhere there is the perfect job that will offer complete fulfillment. It just doesn't work that way, though, and unless our young people confront this reality, they will find themselves four jobs and twenty years later to be very cynical and unsatisfied. This is an accurate picture of millions of men and women in mid-life. To make a living and achieve some sort of status, they have poured all their energies into jobs and routines that are either boring or that they've come to detest. What a tragic and unnecessary waste of undeveloped talent! But it has been demonstrated again and again that when people in their forties, fifties, sixties, and even seventies make a determined effort to channel energies toward developing and expressing latent talent and abilities in creative ways, aside from vocational involvement, boredom, cynicism, and dissatisfaction fade into oblivion. Excitement mounts, and life takes on an aura of exhilaration. Instead of feeling useless in a disjointed world, we begin to feel needed and that we have something that contributes to the well-being of others. And with this discovery comes an interesting serendipity—we're nicer to be around and we stay young longer.

Successful People Don't Judge Their Talent by How Much Money It Earns

One of the saddest spin-offs from the notion that a successful person is one who becomes wealthy and is able to translate that into power and status is the discouragement that comes from unfulfilled dreams. Feelings of failure can cause us to take our talents lightly because we don't earn a lot of money. A person who has the gifts of a teacher and has spent time in preparation and years in the classroom shaping young lives should feel a strong sense of fulfillment, even though the pay may not be large.

It is true, however, that if a person lives in a large city, he or she might quit teaching and get a job with the department of sanitation and earn more money. But would that make him or her more successful? Of course not. It is a tragic distortion of values for any society to give a higher dollar and cents priority to the collecting of garbage than to the training of our children. But the caring teacher recognizes the transient value of a dollar in comparison to educating and giving direction to young people—feeling needed in the use of teaching talent is far more satisfying. By the same token, just because our society is so confused that it heaps more money on a punk rock star for one concert than it does on a doctor who has dedicated his life to medical research doesn't mean the doctor should change vocations. To neglect our gifts because their use would not make as much money is a sin against self and society.

Successful People Find Many Ways To Use Their Talents

Frequently an avocation offers a satisfying outlet for certain of our gifts. Mark Storm is one of the outstanding western artists in the country. His oil paintings hang in a number of galleries and on the walls of many homes and offices, and his bronze sculptures are in demand. He is a human encyclopedia of all things western. But what most people don't know is that while he has always had interest and talent in western lore, most of his life Mark earned his living as a commercial artist. For years he developed his special gift "on the side." He's one of those fortunate persons who came to the place in life where his avocation could become his vocation.

About fifteen years ago, while we were living in New York City, my wife and I went to see the late Will Geer in a tiny theater. He and two other actors were doing "An Evening's Frost." I'm sure that I read Frost in my modern literature class in college, but for all practical purposes this evening was my introduction to the poetry of Robert Frost. I loved it and immediately secured a copy of the complete collection of his work. Across the years I've read and re-read and underlined and memorized lines of his poetry. But I had never read much about him. Just last year Barbara picked up a little biography of Frost. I read it and was amazed to discover that this Pulitzer prize-winning poet, who had read one of his poems at the inauguration of President John F. Kennedy, had earned his living for a large part of his life either farming or teaching school. Somehow knowing the price he had to pay to develop his talent gave new meaning to the words "But I have promises to keep; and miles to go before I sleep" from "Stopping by Woods on a Snowy Evening" *(The Poems of Robert Frost,* New York: Random House, 1946, p. 238).

Then I've known successful people who give expression to their gifts in voluntary service. Henry Woods was a successful engineer with Hughes Tool. But during the time he was using his knowledge and training and skills in one of the major supply companies related to energy development, he also taught a class of boys in his church. He was especially gifted at teaching ten-year-olds, and always built a good relationship with the boys and their families. Among his greatest contributions to the lives of these boys was his gift of showing them how to set goals for their lives.

When Henry reached the mandatory retirement age at Hughes Tool, he was lauded for his contribution to the company, but the people who knew him best felt that while he had served as an excellent employee at Hughes, perhaps his most significant contribution was to the life of the boys in his Sunday school class—his avocation. And since he didn't retire from his teaching, he felt the disadvantages of retirement—from his vocation—less than most people.

Our society is greatly enriched by the people who do volunteer service in hospitals, schools, churches, and charitable organizations. But the people who give of themselves in this way find deep personal joy in their own lives through service to others—there is no satisfaction greater than feeling needed.

As we search for a variety of ways to use our abilities effectively, we will discover that life takes on an exciting zest that banishes boredom and discontent. Our increased involvement multiplies our activities and our feelings of usefulness, and this leads us to assume more responsibility. An intriguing paradox is revealed: *the reward for work well done is more work.* In the story which Jesus told about the landowner and the three men to whom he entrusted capital to be invested, it is interesting that the reward for the two who had done well was to give them more responsibility. That idea seems to contradict the prevailing notion that the reward for work well done is being able to work less. I remember when I was in high school that a good friend of mine suddenly decided that after graduation he was going to join the Navy. When I asked him why, he replied with a glint in his eye, "Don't you see? I'll be able to retire with full retirement at only forty-eight." It was obvious that the most attractive thing about the Navy was being able to retire at a young age.

Recently I was talking to an outstanding young law student who was interviewing for a summer clerking position with a law firm. He had just completed the last of several interviews and had decided to join a certain firm. Since he had previously been offered several job opportunities, I was curious as to what he liked most about the one he had selected, especially since it wasn't one of the largest and most prestigious firms. His answer was concise and somewhat surprising: "This is the only firm where the partners talked to me about their enjoyment of the practice of law. Most of the others focused on the benefits while you practice and on the generous retirement policies." The successful person finds more and more to do and not less and less.

It Isn't How Many Talents We Have; It's How We Use Them

Most of us have experienced times when we have felt that if we had more talent, we would be happy and fulfilled. Then we look around and discover that the majority of the good in the world is being done by people with very ordinary talents but with an extraordinary commitment to developing and using them. The real problem with the man in Jesus' story wasn't that he was given just one talent, but that he didn't use the one he had. We are responsible only for what we do with what we've been given.

Whenever I remember an experience I had at the Grand Ole Opry, I am reminded of the importance of commitment to our gifts. My father loved to listen to country music, and he was a devotee of the Grand Ole Opry. When our family moved from the farm to the city during the depression, Dad got a job at the Farmall shop. With some of the first money he earned he purchased a table model Philco radio. He was attracted to this particular model because, even though we lived in northern Illinois it was guaranteed to bring in the Nashville, Tennessee station which broadcast the Grand Ole Opry.

From that time on our Saturday night ritual was set. Before supper he would tune the radio to the right station. Then he would take the knobs off and put them in his pocket so no one would even be tempted to spoil his evening by changing the station.

Years later when I was speaking at a student convention in Nashville my host casually asked if I would be interested in going to the Opry. I don't think my friend was prepared for such an enthusiastic acceptance. He was an ideal person to take me because he'd lived in Nashville a long time, he knew many of the stars personally, and he promised to take me backstage to meet them. When we were finally seated out front to watch the performance, I confided to my friend that I had been reared on country music and considered myself somewhat of an expert.

One of the first groups was led by a tall lanky man who played the guitar and sang. The announcer called him Sonny James, "The Southern Troubador." He started his half-hour with a song I'd never heard before. As he strummed the guitar and started to sing, the audience began to clap and yell. I wasn't too impressed, and as he finished, I leaned over to my friend and with a condescending tone in my voice I said, "That one won't make it." I had hardly gotten the words out of my mouth when the announcer thanked him for his great performance and announced that the song we had just heard was on his new "gold record." That same thing happened several times during the evening, and each time I was guilty of putting down someone who was already considered a "success." I left the auditorium somewhat confused and very frustrated.

I was still thinking about that experience the next day as I was being taken to the airport by my friend Fred Smith, who at the time was a consultant with Genesco. He asked what I'd done while I was in Nashville, so I told him about my frustrating experience at the Opry. After a time, I said, "You're sort of an expert on things like this. How can a person with such limited ability be so successful?" I have never forgotten his reply, "Kenneth, any person of normal ability or less can be a success in life if he wants to."

After a pause, he continued, "Let me show you the main difference between the musicians you watched and most other people. They have an idea. It's their idea and they don't get tired of it. They stick with it through pie suppers, cake walks, honky-tonks, county fairs, and rodeos until finally one day they are on the stage of the Grand Ole Opry. They've taken their talent to the top." He paused for another moment and then, looking straight at me, he said, "The problem with you and your kind isn't that you don't have any talent. Many of you have gifts those folks on the stage would envy. But, unfortunately, you never take the talent you've been given and devote your whole life to developing it and using it. Most of the good in the world is done by people with ordinary talents who possess an extraordinary commitment to using those gifts."

4

You May Not Be Perfect, But You Can Be Real

IT'S IMPOSSIBLE to have a truly successful life without being a "real" person. One of the greatest compliments that can be paid a person is to say that he or she is "an authentic human being." On the other hand no more damning criticism can be leveled than the suggestion that a person is phony, plastic, or unreal. There are a lot of things I would be interested in being or doing which are beyond my reach through no fault of my own. But we are all plagued with certain limitations which are placed upon us by our background, our gifts, and even the time in which we live. However, each of us, no matter who we are, *can become* an authentic person.

Several years ago there was a song which was very popular, and I still hear it occasionally. The opening lyrics went something like this: What the world needs is love, but that's the only thing there's too little of. Certainly, no one would question the need for love—it is basic to us all. But there is, I believe, another need which we all feel but don't know much about: What the world needs now is "real" people.

There is an interesting fact of life at work that, in our busyness, we may overlook. Unless we are authentic we won't like ourselves, and we aren't comfortable with other people. Authenticity is the basis of all good communication and is the foundation for healthy relationships. It's easier to solve problems and relate well with real people. In my work as a minister I know a lot of very authentic folks. These people are fun to be with, they help me enjoy life more, and just knowing them causes me to feel better about myself. But then I also know many people who aren't real. Being around them is always a discouraging and depressing experience which subtracts a little from life and diminishes me as a person.

While I'm not able to define in a few words the underlying difference between a real person and a phony, I have come to see that there are some things that authentic people are doing that phony and plastic people aren't doing.

Real People Accept Where They're From but Are Unafraid To Grow

I enjoyed the television series which was developed from Alex Haley's book *Roots.* It is a powerful story and carries a profound message for all of us irrespective of our skin color. With heartrending detail, this story seems to focus on the idea that we are not to be ashamed of our beginnings—of who and what we are.

I was born in the front bedroom of a frame house that still stands near the Illinois River in Cherokee County, Oklahoma. My parents farmed a piece of land they rented, and we lived in the house that came with the place. As a little boy, I enjoyed the garden, the cows, the little chickens, and the endless and varied activities that were a part of farm life. And when I started to school, it was in a one-room school house where my teacher taught all eight grades. This was the only world I knew, and I felt good about it.

When I was eight years old, my father gave up farming during the depression of the 1930s and moved our family to the quad-cities area of Northern Illinois where he got a job with one of the major farm implement companies. It was then I found out that I was an "Okie," because that's what the kids in my new school called me. When I asked my mother if I were an Okie, she laughed and said, "Sure, an Okie is someone from Oklahoma." From her perspective that settled it, but I was still bothered because I knew from the tone the kids were using that they thought an "Okie" was someone not quite as good as they were. This made me feel lonely and rejected, and I remember thinking, "I wish I came from some place else." Then, since I was too young to realize what was happening to me, I tried to handle my own insecurities and rejection by tossing put-down expressions at the kids that would make them feel like I did when they called me an "Okie"—words like *Polack, greaser, nigger,* and *wop.* But I remember that trying to put them down didn't make me feel any better about being from Oklahoma.

Years later, when I was a sophomore in college, I was having lunch with a very good friend. In the course of our conversation I began to complain about where I was from and how I had been raised. Without realizing it, I had apparently done this before because Louise stopped me in the middle of a sentence and said, "Kenneth, let me give you a little unsolicited advice. I've listened to you feel sorry for yourself because of where you're from, and about your parents, and about your having arthritis. You didn't pick your parents or where you were born or even the things which have happened to you. But that's the only background you're ever going to have, and I don't think you'll ever be happy until you can accept that fact without apology." Her words took me by surprise, but deep down I knew that she was right. That one conversation laid the foundation for my being able to claim my heritage.

An interesting thing happened after that which surprised me. As time passed and the more comfortable I was with my background, the easier it became to accept it objectively. Then I was able to see and isolate those areas of my life where I needed to grow. Once I accepted where I was from, I was free to reject certain attitudes and values of my upbringing without denying my roots.

Real People Have To Grow Up and Leave Home

To become an authentic person it is necessary for us to move from the dependence relationship of childhood to becoming an independent adult. And this involves much more than just growing older and moving out of our parents' home.

During the last several years, I've been especially aware of how important this is in establishing and maintaining a good marriage relationship. While a very successful marriage and family therapist and I were visiting one day, we talked about some of the most persistent causes of tension between parents and grown children. I was rather surprised when he said, "One of the major contributing factors to this sort of tension in the families I'm seeing is that the parents never really left home emotionally, and they, in turn, are unwilling to turn loose of their children."

Growing up means becoming internally controlled instead of externally managed. It's a part of God's plan for children to be guided toward self-discipline by the loving discipline of parents. Ideally, when a person moves outside the "managing control" of parents, then that person ought to be self-disciplined. Unfortunately, though, the young person who strains against parental guidance with the feeling he will be glad when he's his "own boss" does not really know how to boss himself. So as soon as possible, he replaces his parents with peers, but he is still being controlled externally. During this time, however, a person can actually live with the illusion of independence while continuing to develop an even greater dependence upon externals. A major weakness in our culture today can be traced, I believe, to the fact that we have grown soft and have failed to develop an inner core of values and beliefs which enable us to function as mature adults.

Growing up means moving from reaction to response. Whether we are dealing with our parents, our religion, or our culture a vital part of establishing our identity as real persons is in the process of reacting and questioning the realities of our life. Questioning and reacting is a normal part of the growth process and ought not to concern us unduly, unless it becomes an overall pattern for our life. And if this happens, it becomes a sickness. For example, there are grown men and women who, for an entire lifetime are crippled by reaction to their parents, and I run into people every day who define their religion by what they don't believe. I can understand the problem because it took a very traumatic experience in my life to make me realize my need to move from being the reactor to being the affirmer.

In my late thirties I left a teaching position in a seminary in Ft. Worth, Texas, and accepted an appointment with a seminary in Louisville, Kentucky. Between appointments, however, I spent a year at Union Theological Seminary in New York City as a visiting scholar, studying church patterns in urban America.

I can still recall the culture shock I felt when we moved

to New York City and I became involved in all of the courses related to my subject of study. Quite frankly, I had looked forward to a more open atmosphere. But I was completely unequipped for what I experienced.

As a young professor in Texas there had been a lot of "givens" I could just assume: the church, an evangelical theology, and the need for world evangelization. No one in my circle even thought about challenging these accepted beliefs. Consequently, I busied myself criticizing the tendency of the church to institutionalize itself and exposing some of what I felt were unhealthy trends in evangelism. While much of what I was saying was true and needed to be said, it still made me a reactor, and my agenda was controlled by what others did and by what I reacted to.

But none of the things I had been reacting against in Texas was assumed by the people I was with in New York. For example, I had wanted the church to be more open to change, but here I was sitting in classes with professors and students who weren't sure we should even keep the church. Responsible evangelism was a top priority of mine, but these people looked upon all efforts at evangelism with condescending pity at best and with anger at worst. In fact, several people asked me if I wasn't embarrassed that the seminary I was going to named the chair of evangelism in which I would be teaching after Dr. Billy Graham.

I was intrigued by what was happening to me, but gradually I came to see that I was beginning to approach things from a different direction. Instead of concentrating on what I didn't like, I began to talk about what I believed. No longer was I concentrating on what I wanted to get rid of. Rather, I began to push for what needed to be kept. It was a different posture for me, but it was healthy because it forced me to begin growing up.

And growing up means assuming responsibility for our

lives—for what we believe and what we do. This creates a whole new basis for relating to family, friends, and society. Responsible response is always superior to predictable reaction. Once we "leave home" in any part of our life, we are free then as authentic persons to renegotiate at a more mature level all those relationships which make life enjoyable. Right now, my wife Barbara and I are trying hard to turn loose of our children with grace and a little style. We are not always successful, but we are working hard at knowing and accepting them as adults and relating to them as independent persons. Somehow, we believe, this promises to be the best relationship of all, and it is certainly the most real.

Real People Strive for Consistency

Real people try to be consistent irrespective of where they are or who they are with. This is not easy today for any of us because our lives tend to be so fragmented that we always live with the temptation to be different persons in the many "worlds" in which we live. I've known people who thought they could be ruthlessly ambitious at the office, gentle and loving in the home, and reverent in worship on Sunday without ever mixing the roles or becoming confused about identity. But it just doesn't work.

The foundation for consistency is honesty; honesty with ourselves and with others. Outright stealing and the blatant misrepresentation of facts is costing American taxpayers billions of dollars a year. And not taking seriously the "thou shalt not bear false witness" of the Ten Commandments is exacting a frightful toll in our society. Certainly the bleak and dreary days of Watergate and Abscam bear glaring testimony to a crisis in morals that pervades our culture. And while I'm not a 1980s caricature of Jeremiah, the games we play in so much of modern government and business and as individuals with such agencies as the Department of Internal Revenue gives indication of a shabby disregard for the biblical concept of honesty and truth. The white collar juggling of figures has become a national pastime and signals a breakdown in basic moral values that has cast a noxious pall over our society.

Several years ago I was a guest at a bankers' convention banquet at which Leon Jaworski was the speaker. I was especially anxious to hear him because of his involvement in several very significant and highly publicized hearings as a special prosecutor and also because he has become a symbol for integrity in the law profession. Mr. Jaworski spoke that night with passionate intensity on the subject of honesty. And in the course of his speech, he insisted that there can be no integrity to government or private relationships if people do not tell the truth. To many people, that may seem like a grossly naïve and simplistic statement in view of the complexities in modern society. But the fallacy to this kind of thinking is that basic values of right and wrong, of truth and honesty, do not shift with the winds of our culture. It seems clear to me now that the cure for our "honesty sickness" involves far more than assent to a code of values or even to the words that make it up; it also includes our attitudes, our feelings, and our actions—our total person. It involves discarding our phony piety and shifting ethics in favor of being real people.

Being consistent is easier if we don't try to please everyone. And yet there is nothing more natural than wanting to always please other people. On the other hand, nothing will create more stress and tension than trying to please everyone. It might be easier if we could be like the rabbi who was asked to intervene in a difference of opinion by two women. After the first woman stated her case, the rabbi said to her, "You're right." Then the second woman gave her side of the story, and the rabbi said, "You're right." When a bystander who had witnessed the entire incident stated indignantly, "Rabbi, they can't both be right," he turned to him and said, "You're right, too." There is just no way we can agree with everyone and please them and be real, authentic people.

The desire to have people like us is so strong that if we are not careful, we will find ourselves going against our own values in order to please them. On the surface this may seem to work for a time, but ultimately the duplicity will cause us to lose our self-respect and make us feel phony. One day I heard a speech by a very attractive young woman who was associated with PDAP, a drug rehabilitation group that has been very successful with youth who get involved with drugs. My first thought was that she had probably studied social work in college and had taken the position with the agency because of her interest in helping young people. But I was surprised to learn in the course of her speech that she had come to the agency in the first place as a teenager who was hooked on drugs and had to have help. Then after she had gotten her life straightened out, she stayed on as a staff member in order to do what she could to persuade young people not to get involved with drugs at all and to help those who were already hooked.

After the meeting I had the chance to meet the young woman and visit with her privately. She told me that she had come from a good home, and she excelled as an "A" student until she began using drugs heavily. When I asked her why she had gotten involved with drugs, she answered, "I know exactly why I did it." Then with openness and honesty she explained, "I knew from the beginning that I shouldn't get involved. But most of the people in my group at school were smoking pot, and every time we were together they tried to get me to try it. I didn't even like it at first because it made me sick. But I stuck with it because I felt they would like me more if I did, and more than anything else, I wanted them to like me."

But we will find it much easier to be consistent if we have an inner core of firm beliefs, of standards, and live by them as best we can instead of always having to poll the crowd and then respond to their expectations. To have a set of beliefs that we stick with is like having a moral gyroscope deep down inside. Just as the gyroscope in the ocean-going liner gives it stability even in rough water, our deeply held beliefs allow us to remain secure and purposeful around people who hold different values.

It is virtually impossible, however, to be a member of any group or organization for very long without running into honest differences of opinion. When most any project or plan comes up, some of the group will be for it and others will oppose it. But usually those on both sides of the fence are able to clearly state the reasons for their differences, while at the same time maintaining a healthy respect for each other. However, in most groups there are also those who would like to be on both sides because they don't want to risk the possibility of offending anyone. And it is this fear that provides the excuse for not committing themselves. Fence sitters are usually not effective or happy people. It just isn't real to strive for consensus at the expense of consistency.

Real People Accept the "Givens" but Resist the Stereotypes

To "accept the givens" means to be comfortable with the facts about who we are, what we've decided to do, and the roles we play. For example, I am male by birth, a minister by calling and vocation, and a husband and father by choice. I'm fifty-five years old. These are the givens which relate to my sexuality, my vocation, my marriage, and my age. Unless I can accept this, I will not be a very happy, productive, real person. Unfortunately, though, there is a growing tendency for people to resist the "givens" and accept the stereotypes.

Many of us start out in life with the notion that we are entirely on our own and that how we think, feel, and act is up to us. But we soon discover that many different people were involved in the development of what we are to become. And we are fortunate when we have loved ones and friends who free us to develop our uniqueness and who help us to recognize and develop our particular gifts. On the other hand, there is nothing more stifling to our development and creativity than being forced to accept a stereotype of life. If we want to be real, we will resist them like a plague.

The variety of stereotypes is endless, but let's take a look at just a few. We are confronted every day by sexual stereotypes. Our maleness and femaleness came from God in creation, but a lot of the current attitudes and attributes we've labeled masculine or feminine did not originate with God but are the results of our own delusions. There are all sorts of foolish ideas prevalent today about what men or women are supposed to be interested in, skilled at, or able to do. The stereotype insists that men don't sew, but my tailor is a man. I have an engineer friend who would rather do needlepoint than work crossword puzzles. And recently I performed a wedding ceremony in which the bride, a very feminine young woman, was an engineer with a major oil company. It was interesting to overhear the reactions of people at the wedding reception as they commented on her vocation. After all, "everyone knows women don't make good engineers."

This is about as absurd as the myth that "women don't think logically and are the weaker sex." And it is this same kind of fuzzy thinking that says to a boy who is really hurt, "Be a little man and don't cry."

The job or professions stereotype is one I've always disliked intensely because it tends to dehumanize people. I resist with a passion the usual ministerial stereotype. As a young minister, I soon learned to resist the efforts of people to fit me into a preconceived mold and then apply pressure to get me to conform. Our authenticity, irrespective of job or profession, comes from bringing to our calling our own unique gifts, interests, and experiences, but it also comes from attention to our differences—the places where we just might make our greatest contribution. Being real calls for resisting the mold that would make us exactly like everyone else. I just don't believe God wants us to be stamped out by some celestial cookie cutter.

I believe, too, that we can be more real and our lives will be richer by resisting the age stereotype. Every stage and age of life has its potential for excitement and creativity. I participated recently in a seminar for persons over sixty. Our first speaker was a psychiatrist who had spent years studying people over sixty. He insisted that one of the cruelest forms of prejudice in our society is "ageism"—a negative and distorted feeling about aging. He believes that many of the characteristics we have come to associate with the elderly are imposed on them in the form of an expectation. During the discussion period that followed his talk, vigorous feelings of resentment were expressed about our predilection for judging people and their reactions on the basis of age. Their reaction has made me more sensitive to my own attitudes, and I'm learning to treat those who are my seniors in age with more interest and respect. And my own life is being enriched by this new awareness.

I have come to believe that probably nothing is more damaging to our peace of mind than not recognizing or not being willing to accept our limitations. This is a continuing struggle for me, and I haven't found any easy answers. But as I've worked at it, I have discovered some ways of coping with the problem that have helped me.

Probably one of the first hurdles I've had to overcome in accepting my limitations is to get over the idea that I am the creator and not just a creature. The struggle to "know what God knows" has been going on since the Garden of Eden, and it is essentially an unwillingness on our part to accept the fact that we are creatures and not the creator.

The creator-complex shows itself in many ways. For years in spite of efforts to break the habit, I have tended to accept more responsibilities than I can handle. Even though I say, "No, thank you," more often than, "Yes, I will," I still end up with more commitments than I can possibly handle. Because of this it seems that I'm either late for meetings or miss them entirely, my manuscripts are usually late to the publisher, and I'm unable to really implement the plans and projects that I've made. This is horribly frustrating, and I carry around an overload of heavy feelings of guilt.

One day I asked a friend who knows me well why he thought I continued to overload myself, "Is it that I'm the only one who is really concerned?" He grinned and said half-jokingly, "Your problem isn't that you're too concerned. You just haven't accepted the fact that you are *one* person and that you're not God." His keen perception started me thinking about that. I've got years of conditioning to overcome, but I'm working on it. On Sunday morning before I leave the house for the church the last thing I do is say a little prayer. It always begins with:

O God, thou are the creator and I am the creature,
Thou art infinite and I am finite,
Thou art holy and I am a sinner,
Thou art eternal and I am a mortal.

When the full meaning of those words seeps through into every cell of my body, I'll be on the way to being happier and more real.

We don't all have the same gifts or background or experience. A healthy acceptance of this fact does not represent a cop-out but a realistic way of looking at our own uniqueness and the contribution we can make to life. And it is our differentness that adds to our effectiveness. The Apostle Paul wrote to some Christians who were troubled because everyone didn't do the same thing. He compared the family of God to a body that had many parts but functioned under a basic unity. Paul pointed out how ridiculous it would be if everyone were an eye or a foot. This whole idea has freed me to accept the fact that what may appear to be a limitation created by my particular gifts, background, and experience is, instead, the freedom to use what I have and what I've learned, and all that I've experienced to help other people.

Time limitations afflict all of us. Most people kiddingly talk about needing a "day stretcher" to get their work done. But most of us are also feeling the need of a "life stretcher." The preoccupation with youth and the myths we create about the aging process are but thinly disguised efforts not to accept our time limitations. But it isn't just the "three score and ten" that's hard to accept. It is difficult for us to accept all the other limitations—time with our children, time with our parents, the time we have until retirement. These are all facts of life which confront us—to suppress them can lead to emotional and physical sickness. But to accept the limitation of time in our daily activities frees us to live life fully and with zest.

Real People Show Discernment in Their Meaningful Relationships

Every day of our lives we come in contact with and relate to all sorts of people. And among them we will occasionally discover a person who somehow makes us feel unique and special—the way God intended for us to be. I have a friend who is a secretary, and even though Kathy is quite young, her circle of friends is amazingly broad in age, background, education, and social status. Everyone seems to like her and enjoy being with her. From time to time I've heard speculation as to what it is that attracts people to her. Obviously, there are many factors involved, but I'm convinced that it's because she makes people feel good about themselves when they are with her. Kathy is a very real person, and this has freed her to be an affirmer of others.

By contrast, though, we frequently are with people who have such negative feelings about themselves and others that they drag us down. If allowed to do so, their attitudes will infect ours and make us less real. I know a woman who turned down an excellent position as the executive assistant to one of the officers of a large corporation. On the surface it looked like a great opportunity. But after she'd taken a different position, I asked her why she turned the other job down. Her answer was very perceptive, "When I was with the man I would have worked with, I felt less like a person and more like a thing, and I just didn't want to do that to myself no matter what the job paid."

Obviously, in the give-and-take of daily life we can't avoid this type of person entirely. But as we establish long-term, meaningful relationships, we should deliberately avoid people who make it difficult for us to be our real selves. We can't expect our friends and loved ones to agree with us all the time, but we have every right to want them to accept us as we are and affirm us as persons of worth. One day a young woman, within months of her wedding, came to my office very upset over a "little problem" that she wanted settled before the wedding. She said, "My boy friend is trying to change me." At first I interpreted this as nothing more than pre-wedding nervousness. But as she continued, I could see that he really had begun a campaign to change almost everything about her. Then I told her firmly that she should break the engagement and tell him to find someone who was already molded to fit his likes and dislikes.

Being real is hard enough for most of us when all our close friends and loved ones are encouraging us. But if someone close, whether mate or friend, is always raising questions and is chipping away at us and our self-esteem, it is utterly impossible to be a happy, authentic, and real person.

Real People Are Goal Oriented

In thinking about this, the first thing we need to do is overcome a common stereotype of the goal-oriented person. At least this is true in my case because I tend to think this is a synonym for the "fiercely ambitious" person who would go after what he wants irrespective of who it hurts or what it costs. But now I've come to see that this kind of uptight, desperate, highly motivated climber does not typify authentic people who are goal oriented.

I now see that a truly goal-oriented person is one who has discovered God's purpose and meaning for his or her life, and is then simply implementing decisions for reaching the overall goal. For example, one of the great communicators in this country for the past half century has been Dr. Norman Vincent Peale, pastor of Marble Collegiate Church in New York City and publisher of *Guideposts* magazine. But when I was a young seminarian, I heard a constant flow of carping criticism of Dr. Peale by other ministers because of the positive thinking aspect of his ministry.

But then, several years ago I was Dr. Peale's host at a luncheon where he addressed a number of the heads of corporations in our city. As we visited before the meeting, I asked him to tell me why he went the direction he did in his ministry. He said, "It's very simple. As I was going to the various service clubs to speak, I discovered how very few of the leading businessmen of the community went to church. I was deeply disturbed about this and gave it a great deal of thought and prayer. Eventually I came to a clear conviction that God wanted me to take the church's message to the business community and to the business person whom the church was missing. That was the hard decision. All the other things I've done have simply been efforts to implement that decision."

When, in my late teens, I came to feel God's purpose for my life was to be a minister, I was very excited. But as I began to focus on the reality of uncertain health and on all the years of preparation for which I had no promise of financial support, I began to have grave doubts. So I arranged to spend the night with my Uncle Doc. He was a country preacher, the pastor of a small rural church, and supported himself by farming and carpentering. Uncle Doc had entered the ministry late in his life, and though he lacked formal training, he was a wise man in spiritual matters.

After supper, when Uncle Doc and I were alone, I poured out all the doubts and misgivings I was having about my vocational choice. He listened patiently and asked a question now and then to make sure he understood what I was thinking. Finally, he ended all my struggle with this reassurance: "Kenneth, the God who calls people to do things and be things is a very good person, and he isn't going to put in your heart the dream unless he intends to put within your reach the possibility for fulfilling that dream." We can accept his goals for our lives with confidence. We're not perfect, but we can be whole and real people.

5

Surviving in a Materialistic Society

When I was eight years old, we lived in the country in northeast Oklahoma, and I remember with warm feelings of nostalgia the many times I would slip away alone to my favorite spot on the creek. Armed only with a pocketknife, a string, and one eagle-claw fishhook, I'd cut a willow stick for a fishing pole, and for bait I used "crawdad tails," grasshoppers, or worms, depending upon what the fish were biting and what I could find. And when I got hungry, I could always find tender wild onions in the spring, wild plums in the summer, or persimmons in the fall after the first frost.

The little creek began as a spring behind our house and ran into the Illinois River less than two miles from its point of origin. But that creek meant as much to me as the mighty Mississippi did to Mark Twain; it was my world to explore. At times when the fishing was slow I would dream about faraway places and of doing adventuresome things. There was no limit to the range of my imagination—everything began along that little creek and then moved out to and beyond the Illinois River. I didn't understand fully many of my dreams or the implication of all that I was learning along that creek-bank. But in some mysterious way, it seemed to me even then that I was being equipped for living in that larger world.

When we moved to an industrial city in northern Illinois, my love for the world of nature led me to become a Boy Scout. And while the uniforms, extensive equipment, and manuals seemed to be excess baggage to me, I was drawn like a gnat to the light by the chance to camp out in a wilderness environment. Among other things, I remember vividly the traditional "two-match" fire, and I can still feel the surge of pride and accomplishment when I succeeded in lighting a fire without a match.

Even though those experiences occurred forty and more years ago, there's still a lot of that little boy in me. I'm intrigued by stories of people surviving in a wilderness setting because they know which wild plants and berries are safe to eat and which might poison them—which animals, insects, and snakes are harmful and which are safe. This is all part of the fascinating art of knowing how to survive in a hostile environment.

In recent years I've come to realize that all of us face challenges in our lives which make it necessary for us to develop survival techniques. There was a period in my life when I assumed, naïvely, that the world in which I lived would be completely friendly to my efforts to build a successful life. But I have come to see that this simply isn't true. While I am not a prophet of gloom and doom, I do believe that we—all of us—strive to live the successful life in the context of a hostile environment. Such being the case, we must learn just what will nourish our dreams as opposed to what will destroy them.

Within the boundaries of the hostile environment in which we all live, there are numerous forces which, if given the chance, can thwart and strangle our efforts to be useful and successful persons. And perhaps one of the most destructive of these forces is the love for, and intense preoccupation with, material gain. This kind of compelling drive can so discolor and distort our sense of values that we become unaware we are off track and our lives have lost that creative relationship with God so essential to real success. Ironically, we usually recognize the obsession with material things in others, but do not see it in ourselves. In this part of life, as in others, so often we hide the truth with our rationalizations.

One of the most fascinating stories Jesus told is about a man referred to as the "rich young ruler." In fact, the disciples were so impressed by this unusual story that it shows up in three of the Gospels. It is impossible, of course, for us to slip back in time and know for sure the feelings and thinking of this young man. But I think the story gives us enough hints into his character to assume that if Jesus had asked him to rate on a scale of one to ten the relative importance of family, God, and what he owned, he would have rated God and family way above his possessions. However, his mask fell off under the penetrating eyes of Jesus, and he learned to his sorrow that the real love of his life was what he had acquired materially and that these possessions had now come to control him. He had let himself be deceived into thinking that he was a righteous man interested in the spiritual life and discovered, instead, he was a materialist.

We all feel the pressures, from outside as well as from within, to place an excessive value on the acquiring of material things—we belong to certain clubs, drive big cars, live in the "right" neighborhoods, as one means of impressing our peers. At the same time, having and doing these things frequently causes a false sense of self-worth.

How can we handle these pressures? One way, I believe, is to establish an authentic rationale for not giving top priority to making money for the purpose of acquiring material things and translating that into power and status. As I have worked on this in my own life, I've discovered some things that have been helpful to me.

Our condition at both birth and death makes a strong argument against spending life's best energies accumulating things.

Almost two thousand years ago an elderly minister wrote these words to a young friend, "We brought nothing into the world; for that matter we cannot take anything with us when we leave" (1 Tim. 6:7, NEB). Dr. Charles Allen is one of the best communicators in our country whether he is speaking before a group or writing his newspaper column or doing a book. Recently, he made a classic comment about our obsession with making money and accumulating today's symbols of affluence and wealth—a unique twist to the old "You can't take it with you" idea, "Have you ever seen a hearse with a U-haul trailer behind it?"

Our real needs are very simple. For our bodies *we need* food, clothing, and shelter. For our spirits *we need* a few people to love us, work that is challenging, and a relationship with God. Usually, tension bends us painfully, and our sense of purpose and meaning becomes confused when we can't distinguish between what we *want* and what we really *need.* When we're tempted by a distortion of wants and needs, most of us would benefit by a vivid memory-resurrection of those times when we had much less and our needs were far simpler.

Now, all of our children are in college or graduate school. As we live their experiences with them, I'm reminded of my own college days—some memories are happy, others are painful. But perhaps the most vivid memory involved money. It just didn't seem to stretch as far as my needs. At first I always ran out of food money before my next payday, and this played havoc with my ability to concentrate and study. Fortunately, about that time I read an article describing the nutritional value of peanut butter. I liked peanut butter and it was cheap then, so on my next payday I bought a quart jar of peanut butter and a two-pound box of crackers and stashed them on the top shelf in the closet. From then on, when my money ran out, instead of heading for Jake's Grill with the fellows, I would hole up in my room with peanut butter and crackers and study. My body didn't seem to suffer too much, and my grades were certainly helped by the extra time for study. It was a survival technique I used all the way through college and seminary. One thing is sure—many times I was bored with my menu, but I don't recall ever feeling sorry for myself.

Thankfully, I've had the foresight, though, not to put up my college experiences as models for my own children. I'll admit it's a temptation now and then, but I used to hate the "when I was your age" stories from my parents. So, I don't want to lay that load on young people now. Then, too, I've come to see that I've changed a lot since my "peanut butter and cracker" days. I've moved a lot of the items which were originally on my "want" list over to my "need" list. Many things I considered optional in my life twenty years ago are "standard equipment" now. The years have produced a steady and subtle seepage from my wants to my needs, and I'm beginning to wonder if it isn't time to reexamine my real needs and move toward a simpler lifestyle.

The temptation of materialism is not a new problem, and it isn't likely to go away. It won't be solved by efforts at withdrawal or simplistic ideas. However, I believe it can be managed successfully if we thoughtfully spell out guidelines for checking our attitudes and actions. Creative use of these guidelines will help us break some old habits of thinking and acting and provide insight into the development of new habits. It would also give us a basis for evaluating where we are now and the means for making better decisions for the future. At the same time these guidelines would provide mental, emotional, and spiritual boundaries which would help us see when we've wandered too far out and are wrong and give us assurance and confidence when we are right. And in our attempt to establish these personal guidelines, we will want to set them in view of where we are now but also be aware of the probable need for their modification and expansion for a future lifetime of growth.

As I have wrestled with this very human problem of attempting to discover a proper sense of values and balance in the handling of material things, I've had the opportunity of knowing many people who seemed to have developed a healthy and creative style for coping with the problem. Only a few of these were actually wealthy—most were in the broad middle class range, but some were quite poor. None of them, nor any of us, can escape the pressures of a materialistic society. But, as I have watched these people function in all kinds of circumstances, I've been able to isolate what I believe it is in their thoughts and actions that distinguishes them from those who seem to cave in under the pressures of money and the adult toys and goodies it will buy. In bringing these characteristics together, as I see them, we have a "survival kit" for making it in a materialistic world.

Successful People Face Realistically What Possessions Can and Can't Do

It would be wrong to idealize poverty. Very little good can be said for being poor. And it would be equally wrong to caricature riches as though they were innately wrong. Having money can make an enormous difference in our lifestyles. It cannot only provide the basic needs, but also the comforts, and it can buy the best health care available. When a person is in trouble, money can attract better legal representation than most people can afford. It creates the potential for mobility while the less fortunate are stuck where they are, and wealth can open doors for training and the accompanying opportunities which do not exist for those who have less. Yes, there are a lot of things which money can buy and to pretend it isn't so is absurd.

But it is enormously important to maintain perspective in view of the fact that there are certain things money can't buy. For example, it won't buy *friendship.* I've known wealthy men and women who use their money to surround themselves with people whom they hope are "friends."

But I've discovered that in most cases they live with the haunting question of whether they are liked merely because of their money or for themselves. More than once I've heard the agony of being unsure, filtered through intense feelings of loneliness.

Money won't buy *love.* It will buy sex, and there are some people who still try to pretend that love and sex are the same, but the pretense is painfully hollow. Sex bought, either in marriage or outside of it, is a savage assault on the personhood of everyone involved, and irrespective of the tone of surface communication, underneath it all the feelings are usually contempt, not love.

And money won't buy *respect.* There are people who use money to gain loyalty and deference from others and then pretend this is actually respect for them as persons. But this charade doesn't fool anyone.

Money cannot buy *exemption from the problems* which are common to everyone. While rich people can afford the best medical treatment, they still get sick and have incurable diseases. Recently, one of the most prominent families in South America brought a beautiful child who had a very advanced form of cancer to the Medical Center in Houston in hopes of finding a cure. Somehow I was able to feel the enormous frustration of that family whose almost limitless resources were impotent to help this little one they loved so much.

The children of wealthy families can break the hearts of their parents, as can children from the slums. Money, or lack of it, doesn't seem to make any difference. Then, too, money hasn't been particularly effective in holding marriages together. In fact, none of the valuables which give life dimension can be purchased. Character, meaning and direction in life, peace of mind, a sense of fulfillment, understanding and wisdom, and our hope are earned but not bought.

Successful People Learn To Prize Their Non-Material Assets

Perhaps one of the best ways for us to keep life in perspective is to center our attention on the many valuable possessions we have which are non-material. A constant awareness of this can help hold us steady as we move and live in a culture distorted by an almost mad drive to acquire "things"—to achieve affluence at whatever cost.

Recently, I was reminded of the extent of this distortion of values while listening to an on-the-spot television interview with the resident of an apartment that had been devastated by fire. The woman appeared to be in her late thirties or early forties and was understandably distraught. The reporter began the interview with what was meant to be a word of solace, "I guess as bad as it is, you're thankful no one was seriously injured." The woman replied with intense feeling, "I suppose that's the way I'm supposed to feel, but I don't. I lost everything in the world that's valuable to me in that fire."

I'm sure allowances should be made for the understandable hysteria that would overwhelm any of us who lost most, if not all of our material possessions in a fire. But, as I thought about her reactions, I began to suspect that her perceptions—even though she was in shock—mirrored the sentiment that would be expressed by most people in similar circumstances. And then I turned my thoughts inward: What do I have that can't be burned in a fire, stolen by burglars, or listed on a financial statement. It's a list I need to make and keep up to date and enlarge.

We all learn from others if we are open and sensitive to what is going on around us. I did, through the experience of a friend who was a highly successful real estate developer. Bill was a man of character and ability who took risks and worked hard. That combination had made him very wealthy, but at the time of my story he had launched the most ambitious project of his career. Coincidentally, two events occurred which were beyond his control, but which led to the failure of his business—the Middle-East embargo of oil created a debilitating gasoline shortage that caused prices to soar, and then as the economy slowed to a snail's pace, interest rates climbed to an unbelievable high. The cash flow needed to keep the business afloat so exceeded the income that it was impossible to save the business. In a state of shock Bill seriously considered suicide, but before doing anything he went to see a friend of many years for advice and help. "Charles, I've lost everything," he blurted out. "There's nothing left to live for."

Charles listened until he'd heard the whole story several times and then said quietly, "I know you feel like you've lost everything, but from listening to you very carefully, I don't really think you have. For example, what about your wife and children? Have they left you?" Bill was shocked at the thought and quickly responded, "Of course not. My wife is wonderful! She's stuck with me through it all and knows we won't even be able to save the house, but she loves me and is my best supporter."

Then Charles asked, "Bill, you're one of the most talented men I know and have solid experience in your business. Did the bankruptcy court take your ability too?" The response was obvious, and Bill even admitted that through the experience he had probably learned some things that would make him a more capable person.

"Have your friends lost respect for you and turned their backs on you?" By now, Bill was beginning to get the point. He opened up and talked of the deep respect and encouragement he felt from friends who had stood by him and his family.

After they'd talked for a long time, Charles said, "I'm not going to minimize the loss of a business you'd spent years developing, but it seems to me that when a man has the love of a good wife, the respect and best wishes of his friends, and more ability than he had before, he has a few blessings yet to be thankful for." The point was made!

Successful People Try Not To Substitute Material Things for Time, Love, or Self

It is easy for all of us to become victims of the subtle and possibly subconscious notion that there are adequate substitutes for time and love and self which can be bought. I remember so well a time in our lives when I struggled with this. Our children were small, and I was traveling a great deal. This meant that Barbara had to assume most of the parenting responsibility. Probably, from feelings of guilt I got into the routine of "bringing them something" from each trip. I rationalized this as a token of my love for them, but because of my feelings of guilt, it was actually sort of a bribe. This is a familiar trap which a lot of absentee-type parents have fallen into. But after just a few trips home and being greeted by "What did you bring me?" I realized how hollow and superficial our relationship had become. So the next time I came home and the children asked me what I'd brought them, I said, "Me. I've brought you me. I've missed you very much, and I love you."

I still had to be away a lot, but through this experience I learned never to try to substitute a gift for "me." This is one of the hardest lessons we have to learn—the quality of a father's presence means much more to a teenager than the gift of a flashy sports car. And the warmth of a mother's love carries greater lasting worth than the buy-off gift of a new stereo.

This whole idea applies equally well to the marriage relationship. Husbands and wives must never let the gift of things become a substitute for words of appreciation, special times together, interest in each other, and shared feelings. One time on an elevator I heard a man sum up his entire relationship with his wife in two sentences, "I don't know what's wrong with my wife," he said. "I've given her a house, a car, and a handful of credit cards, and she's still not happy." You certainly don't have to be an expert on marriage to figure out that a large part of his problem was that everything he gave her could be bought with money. What she really needed was him—his presence, his ear, his love acted out with something more than his money could buy.

Successful People Learn To Delay Getting or To Do Without Something They Want and Can Afford

On the surface this may seem a little weird and otherworldly. It certainly isn't a pattern of life that is popular in our late twentieth-century world. Billboards, newspaper ads, and countless commercials on radio and television hammer away at our conscious and subconscious minds in a concerted effort to create a desire for products and services. Someone has estimated that the average young person has seen 350,000 commercials by the time he or she graduates from high school. The mood of our culture is that if we want something and can afford it, we should go right out and buy it.

We are all, irrespective of age, assaulted by this philosophy of life, but I think it shows up more destructively with young adults. It seems to me that young people in their twenties and thirties frequently become driven to acquire assets and material things which it took their parents half a lifetime to own. Now, I'm certainly not opposed to the idea that young families should enjoy the benefits and rewards from hard work and professional achievement, but there is a subtle self-gratification itch that can take over if we're not sensitive to it. And when this happens, our sense of values becomes eroded. The compulsion for instant self-gratification becomes the driving force in life, chipping away constantly at our integrity as whole persons. The philosophy of self-gratification as a way of life can be very destructive to our happiness and can keep us from being truly successful.

The best reason I can give for setting some limits on gratifying self is that it breaks what can become a very destructive cycle. There is a strange, very human law at work here—the compulsion to acquire material possessions seems to have a narcotic effect on us. The more we get, the more we want. I was sitting in my office between services one Sunday when one of our members who is outstanding in the field of preschool education dropped by for a moment. She said, "I was over in one of the preschool departments this morning, and I saw an interesting contradiction." It seems that she had stopped by one of the classrooms during refreshment break. At the moment, the children were quietly enjoying a small glass of orange juice and two large sugar cookies. One of the workers for whom the morning had been an ordeal said, "I hope this will calm them down. They've got so much energy they're wearing me out." My friend laughingly concluded, "I didn't have the nerve to tell her that by giving them sugar cookies she was working against herself. Within minutes their little bodies will convert all that sugar into pure energy, and she will be climbing the walls."

I was with Dr. Charles Allen recently and watched him put some young couples into shock as he shared his feelings about the need to place limitations upon themselves concerning going into debt for things. What made it both humorous and sad was that he was articulating a philosophy which was accepted almost without question forty years ago and which would be rejected by the same majority today. He admitted in the beginning that living in a church parsonage meant that he had never had the need to buy a house. They could identify with that because this was a group of young ministers and their wives. But what flipped them was his next statement, "We bought a car on time payments when I finished seminary, and when we finally got it paid for, my wife and I decided that from then on we would not go into debt for anything. If we could not pay for it, we did not buy it." While they were recovering from the shock of what they considered a most radical philosophy, he added with a smile, "And, you know, we discovered very soon that there were a lot of things we could do without."

Successful People Learn the Deep Satisfaction of Giving

Most of us learned this little verse from the Scriptures when we were small: "It is more blessed to give than to receive." But more often than not in the nitty gritty of life this is used as sort of a pious platitude to cover up a disappointment when we didn't receive quite as much as we had given. Very few people actually act as though giving made them happier than receiving. I must confess that though I've given lip service to the blessings of giving, it has only been in recent years that I've had the idea authenticated for me in experience and observation.

I knew when I became a minister that part of my responsibility was to motivate the different members of the church to give their money to take care of the needs of the church. In my role as a member of the church I had no problem with giving. One of the easiest and most satisfying things I did was to give a tenth of my income to the church. It was a different story, though, when I tried to convince others to give proportionately; I was very uncomfortable. But then I began to watch men and women who were givers, not just of money, but of themselves as well, and I saw that they were the really whole and happy people. Slowly, it dawned on me that when I helped people learn to be generous with their money and time, I was really contributing to their potential for a happier and more successful life.

I have a friend who is the epitome of generosity himself, but he has also made a vocation of helping others who are wealthy learn to enjoy sharing their blessings. At his suggestion one of his clients provides his luxurious River Oaks home for the single adults from the church to use for a Christmas party. And my friend has been influential in getting an outstanding businessman interested in the local Christian university. Over the years I've watched him do this sort of thing so often that one day I commented that he had developed to a fine art the ability of getting other people to give their money to causes he was interested in. Howard's reply was, "Kenneth, when I help someone who's skilled at making money, but who hasn't learned the joy of giving it to support the things which help our world, I'm doing him a favor he will always be grateful for." I decided he was right.

Successful People See Themselves Less as Owners and More as Stewards

One of the most deeply rooted instincts we have is to own things large or small and to be able to say "this is mine." These days this is sometimes more of a feeling than a reality when you think of thirty-year loans, balloon notes, and other even more sophisticated and innovative types of financing. However, that in no way detracts from the enjoyment of saying "all of this is mine."

But while there is satisfaction in asserting ownership, there is also the temptation of arrogance. It's not hard to understand how the farmer whose story Jesus told felt intoxicated by his success and began to talk about what to do with "*my* barns." This is a sure signal, though, that true values have been misplaced. Selfish arrogance and a sick pride of ownership seem to produce lonely and unhappy people. By contrast the happiest people I know are those who, in spite of what a title search might reveal, look upon what they own as a sacred trust for which they are responsible.

My friend Ray Graham epitomizes this view of life. He was reared in a large but very poor family, and although he enjoyed high school, Ray had to drop out before graduating in order to help support the family. After a time he went to work for J. C. Penney and became one of the company's outstanding managers.

Ray developed a close lifelong friendship with Mr. Penney himself, and there had been speculation that he would have eventually become president of the company had he stayed with them. But he was more interested in the stability of his family, so he abandoned the frenetic corporate life and opened his own retail clothing store in Houston. Mr. Penney came to the opening of that store to wish him well and to help him dedicate it. By the time I met Mr. Graham he was almost retirement age and had more than a dozen highly successful men's stores in several cities.

One day Ray and I were on a trip together, and I asked him about his habit of having a prayer of dedication each time he opened a new store. I pointed out that stores are more apt to be opened with champagne or a clown than with a prayer. He summed up his whole philosophy of life with these unforgettable words, "I do it to remind myself and those who work for me that though the stores bear my name there is a sense in which I am not really the owner. I'm the steward to whom God has given the responsibility of running them."

Successful People Replace the Love of Things with a Larger Love

Ultimately, taking control of material things is an affair of the heart and not of the head. This is where the allegiances and the priorities of life are settled. One of the disturbing myths about Christianity portrays it as being "other worldly"—unconcerned about what goes on here. But a thoughtful reading of the Gospel stories refutes this silly notion. Again and again we see Jesus helping people who were filled with anxiety about material things. Whenever he came across a person who was all uptight about material things, he gently, but firmly, began trying to get them to revise their priorities. And whenever Jesus encountered a person who had given top priority in life to material possessions, he stressed the necessity of a new focus—a new center. He urged his listeners to "seek first the kingdom of God, *then* these things shall be added." His point was that larger love was capable of putting all other needs into proper perspective.

It is important for us as Christians to stop treating covetousness as though it were some minor flaw. Inordinate desire, which is what covetousness means literally, is a violation of the tenth commandment. And in the New Testament covetousness is treated as a synonym for idolatry—a violation of the commandment to not have other gods. This idolatry makes us insensitive to the needs of others, blinds us to our own condition, deludes us about our own mortality, justifies all kinds of evil, and cuts us off from the voice of God.

The people I know who have been able to manage living successfully in a materialistic society are those who have allowed God to fill their lives with a larger, more powerful, and more satisfying love. When this happens an amazing paradox takes place—the person who allows the love for possessions to be replaced by a larger love seems to discover a greater capacity for enjoying those material things. They are more comfortable with themselves and others, with God and his demands, and with the world in which they live. But we will never become truly successful persons until we have been set free from the tyranny of things, and have discovered, through the liberation Jesus Christ alone can give, the ability to survive in a materialistic world.

6

Managing Our Fears

FEAR IS THE EMOTIONAL reaction usually caused by the presence or possibility of danger, evil, harm, or great misfortune, whether real or imagined. It is an emotion that is with us constantly at every stage of life, and if left uncontrolled, can strip us of our sense of well-being and happiness. Uncontrolled fears and anxieties are one of the greatest roadblocks to a successful life.

Fear Undermines Trust

Fear undermines trust which in turn affects all of our relationships. While I was in college, a minister whom I'd come to love and admire was fired by his congregation. Actually, he was allowed to resign, but if he had refused, they would have dismissed him. I was devastated by this event because of concern for my friend, and for the first time I felt threatened about my own security as a future minister. But when I learned several weeks later that he had been called to a good church in South Texas, I was delighted because he had so much to give. And I felt that once again his gifts and talents would be used to help people. To me it seemed that he had been given a chance to forget the past and to start over again with life. I was too young and inexperienced to realize what the experience had done to him and to his wife and children.

Later, when I moved to Texas to attend seminary, he invited me to come to his church and preach for a special week of youth services. I accepted gladly and looked forward to being with him again. When I arrived, I was thrilled—it was a large and influential church. The congregation was made up of gifted and committed members who had a genuine appreciation for their pastor and for the leadership he was giving the church. It seemed a perfect place in which to find healing for his scars.

But one night during the early part of the service he said something to me that made me realize that the terror of having been fired had created a dread which made him unable to trust people whom he had known before his experience. As we were going to the platform, I shared with him some compliments I had heard about his work and said that I could see he was really loved and appreciated. There wasn't time for him to respond immediately, but during the offertory he leaned over and said, "You're probably right about the people's feelings toward me, but I need to tell you my feeling about them. I know it's wrong and I've tried to change, but each week as I sit here and observe them, my mind is haunted by the question, 'Will they stand with me or against me when there's trouble?' " His fear was like a treacherous undertow which kept pulling him down, and it blocked the rebuilding of his life.

Fear Distorts Our Problems

Fear has a way of magnifying and distorting all our problems. When I was nine years old, a small carnival came to our little town, and in exchange for helping the sign painter I was given a free pass to all of the amusements and rides. The show I kept going back to more often than any of the others was the House of Mirrors—nothing looked the way it really was, and I thought the distortions were hilarious. As I look back on the experience now, I can see that being controlled by fear is like taking our troubles into a house of mirrors where they immediately are given new and formidable proportions.

One of the tragic events in Israel's history is a reminder of what fear can do to our perspective. They were all poised to cross over the river and enter the promised land after traveling through the wilderness from Egypt. A twelve-man committee had been sent on ahead and had spent forty days on a reconnaissance mission, and when they returned, ten of the men gave a report that was warped by fear. While admitting that the land was rich and did indeed "flow with milk and honey," they alarmed everyone with the report that the people were like "giants." In fact, they went so far as to say that the Israelites "seemed like grasshoppers" in comparison. The other8 two, however, were not fearful and urged the Israelites to enter the land immediately with the confidence that God would be with them. But the fear of the ten spread like a plague and the people panicked. They turned back into the arid desert for many years of aimless wandering and death. Fear always paralyzes and is a dangerous emotion to mix with any problem.

We are less able to handle the risks if fear takes control. So often our preoccupation with "playing it safe" replaces striving to find the best way to accomplish things, and we spend too much energy spreading the responsibility so there will be no one to blame if something goes wrong. There is nothing new about this kind of fear. Jesus was familiar with it because he talked about it in the story of the one servant who, because of fear, buried his one talent instead of investing it wisely. He was afraid to risk, and in the process everything was lost. Fear can make us afraid to risk in relationships, in our work, and in our religion.

The list of what fear can do to our lives seems endless. In its mildest form it can create a kind of uneasiness about our lives which diminishes everything, and in its most savage form, fear is capable of immobilizing us and rendering us incapable of functioning in any area of our lives. This is why it is so important that each of us learn to look carefully at those things we are afraid of and find ways for managing them. I purposely used the word "manage" in preference to "solve," because we never completely get rid of fear in our lives. Like temptation, it will always be with us, and we must learn to cope with it.

So many of the fears which have haunted people across the centuries no longer exist, but fear continues to grip us even in today's world. That seems like a paradox because we live in miracle times. Just a little less than five hundred years ago sailors were afraid they would fall off the edge of the earth, but in our lifetime we've watched men on the moon, and our scientists are sending television signals to Saturn. Today we have sufficient knowledge of the nature of creation to no longer be captive to the primitive fears that the rocks and trees and rivers contain evil spirits that will attack us. Medical knowledge has taken such giant strides during this century with immunizations, antibiotics, and new skills in surgery that many dread diseases have been eliminated. Advanced technology in agriculture has opened the way to produce crops of a quantity and quality to feed even the exploding population of today's world. And much of the guesswork is taken out of weather predictions by the use of satellites that circle the globe and send back accurate data. But in spite of all these advances ours is a generation eaten up by fear.

Fear of Rejection

We all fear rejection. The need to be liked and approved of by others is great, but it can cause us to do many things which are actually against our best interests in the long run. Fear of rejection causes us to conform to a group's values and lifestyle even when it violates our convictions. It causes us to mask much of our real feelings about people, ideas, and events for fear they will not be accepted. And the fear of rejection is often the main motivation behind the inordinate desire so many people have to know what is "in" and what is "out," whether it's books, plays, places to ski, clothes, morals, or people.

Phil hit law school with high grades and low self-esteem. His goals were to maintain an average which would qualify him for Law Review and to be liked by his peers. As a child, he had been asthmatic and still had enough allergies that his body had a very low tolerance for many things, one of which was alcohol. His system was so sensitive that one drink made him violently ill. Even though Phil knew exactly what it would do to him, he would go ahead and drink beer with other students on Friday night "just to be sociable." And he suffered through a weekly illness because he was afraid to risk the group's rejection by telling them he could not drink.

Fear of Failure

It's not just recent graduates on their first job who have some anxieties about whether or not they can make it, but everyone involved in a job change—a shift to somewhere else or to assuming a larger responsibility. When I left Atlanta and came to Houston to assume my present position as a pastor of a large church, the fear of possible failure gripped me. After all, my experience had been limited to a student pastorate fifteen years before. And most of the intervening time had been spent as a professor in the seminary classroom. The experience gap I faced gave me some tense moments of anxiety.

We are also afraid of failure in our relationships. Teenagers suffer painful fears as they move from the snug harbor of parent love into the trickier currents of boy-girl relationships. I sense an almost unconscious feeling of anxiety at many weddings. Even behind all the laughter, there seems to be an awareness of a lurking danger illuminated by today's high divorce statistics. Scarcely a week goes by when parents of young children do not make an appointment to see me about the anxiety they are feeling over the responsibility and the challenge of rearing children properly.

I once experienced the fear of failure to such a degree that I almost made a decision which would have impoverished the rest of my life. It was during Thanksgiving week of my second year at seminary that I had my first date with Barbara Burke who was working on a master's degree. It was a different sort of date than I had expected. We got into an argument over something one of my favorite professors had said in a chapel message. I discovered then that it is possible to learn a lot more about a person in a spirited argument than by holding hands at a concert. She had a good mind and was an excellent student; she had strong opinions and was not afraid to express them even when her date didn't agree. I was half mad when I escorted her to the door of Barnard Hall that night, but as I walked down the steps to my car I knew I was hooked.

We began dating with some regularity, and on a small

campus with lots of activities which overlap, it's possible to spend a lot of time together in a relatively short period of time. The more I knew about her, the more I enjoyed her, and as our relationship grew we fell in love with each other. I had the idea of marriage on my mind a long time before I finally proposed, and when I did ask her to marry me late on a Sunday night, she accepted. When I went back to my dorm that night, I was the happiest human being in town.

But I woke up the next morning with the fear of getting married permeating every fiber of my body, but it was not the normal anxiety of a young man about to take the big step. I was so ill physically that I could not go to classes. The seminary doctor did all the routine tests on me and assured me that there was nothing seriously wrong with me. He may have guessed that my illness was caused by some kind of emotional disturbance, but I didn't tell him about my feelings of fear.

Somehow, as I thought about what was happening to me, I knew that it didn't have anything to do with Barbara. She was everything I had ever wanted in the person I hoped to marry. I had no idea where my fear came from, though I thought it could easily have been caused by the stored up pain of my parent's divorce. I did come to see, though, that the thinking and deciding part of me wanted to marry Barbara, but apparently my subconscious was sending up messages full of fear and anxiety: "Marriage is risky; marriage is dangerous; you can't afford a mistake; you shouldn't marry anyone."

The story has a good ending because we were married on July 17, 1954; we have three grown children and an exciting marriage. But I would have missed all of this if I had given in to my fears. It took a very patient Barbara, a wise professor, a God who hears our prayers, some brooding time, and a visit to Barbara's home to exorcise the fears forever. But I have not forgotten what it is like to be held in the grips of a fear I couldn't seem to control.

The Fear of Missing Out on "Life"

This fear permeates all age groups. Some people keep driving themselves to new experiences for fear they will end up on the wrong side of thirty and won't have really lived—a disco they haven't danced in; some restaurant they haven't eaten in; a ski resort they haven't vacationed in; or some new fad they've not gone along with. Frequently, older adults reach the place in life where they should be clipping the coupons which come from a lifetime of wise investment in living. But instead they get caught up in the fear that life has somehow passed them by. They are gripped with the fear that the only way they can possibly be fulfilled is to grab for whatever they think will make them happy without giving any thought to the price.

Cynthia married too young and against everyone's advice, but she and Dick seemed happy, and as the children came along, her parents relaxed a bit and hoped for the best. Dick felt she was a good wife—she was good with the children and seemed to be contented with her life. On her thirty-sixth birthday her friends had a party for her. During the course of the evening an unthinking wag said to her, "Cynthia, you'd better pack a lot of living into these next few years because after you've reached forty you'll be over the hill."

That single statement surfaced the fear that life was passing her by—a fear Cynthia had been nursing on the back-side of her mind for a long time. Each day she stirred the thought in her mind until it became an obsession with her. Finally, six months later she left a "good-bye" note to her husband and children, caught a cab to the Greyhound terminal, and took the bus to Houston, Texas.

Twelve months later Cynthia came to me for help because she had come to the painful decision that the freedom and excitement she had reached for had not been worth the losses she had experienced. After we had visited a while and I had made a commitment to try to help her, I asked her to think back and tell me why she thought she had left her home and family.

"Fear," she said. "I felt like I was growing old too fast; it seemed that I had been married all my life, and the fear that I was missing the 'real' life became an obsession with me. In my desperation I made a decision that has left everyone I love in the world deeply scarred, myself most of all."

The Fear of Making Commitments

On the Sunday Robert and Marion Maddrey celebrated their fifth-fifth wedding anniversary we were invited to have Sunday dinner with them at Bayou Manor. They had reserved the guest dining room off the main hall, and it created a wonderful setting for the ten of us to eat and visit. Besides the Maddreys there were two widows, two couples who had been married fifty years, and us. As we sat there and listened to them reminisce about their wedding, I began thinking about the years of personal commitment to marriage which were represented at that table. With a little figuring I discovered that the ten of us accounted for almost two hundred and fifty years of marriage.

During a lull in the conversation I shared this with them, and someone asked, "Why don't people who get married today have that same long-term commitment?" This was a good question, and after thinking for a few moments, I told them I felt that marriage today was suffering from the same kind of a fear of commitment that infects every area of life—jobs, children, friendships, and church.

There was general agreement that this was probably true. Then one of them, with just a touch of irritation, suggested, "Someone should tell these young people that if they are afraid of commitments, they are afraid of life."

Managing Our Fears

In reflecting on that conversation later, I pondered the question, "What can we do to get control of our fears?" Even as I asked the question, it was obvious that trying to escape from our fears, whatever the method, only makes matters worse, and trying to repress them produces more serious problems for a later time.

I have found great help in managing fears and anxieties from some counsel which Jesus Christ gave. Many of my friends are surprised to discover that Jesus spent a lot of time talking to people about their fears and anxieties. Again and again in the Gospel stories, Jesus speaks to his listeners about their anxieties and fears, and then he gives us this assurance, "Peace I leave with you; my peace I give to you; not as the world gives do I give to you. Let not your hearts be troubled, neither let them be afraid" (John 14:27). Then, too, over the years I've read a lot of books and articles about fear written by experts in the field of mental health and counseling. All of this has been helpful, but nothing I have read surpasses the words of Jesus in the Sermon on the Mount. Like others, I had read the words for years before mining from them practical insights for my daily life. Among the many unforgettable words found in the Sermon on the Mount, I have discovered three key ideas that have helped me.

First, I need to settle the top priority for my life. I memorized "Seek ye first the kingdom of God, and his righteousness; and all these things shall be added unto you" (Matt. 6:33, KJV), long before its message about my fears came through to me. When he said this, Jesus was speaking to destitute people in a very poor land whose anxieties were always centered on survival. Yet to these people whose main concern was whether they would have food or clothing or shelter for their families, he said, "The first thing you need to do is to push all those fears aside for a moment and settle what will be *first* in your life."

His call to discipleship always demands a shifting of all our priorities. And any response to that call which merely causes us to join a church without a refocusing of our lives has missed the point of Jesus' teaching. He makes it clear that our allegiance to him must take precedence over every other relationship in life. In Luke 14 Jesus states unequivocally that we are to put him above our families, our possessions, or even above our own selves.

Unfortunately, this revolutionary idea has lost its impact because of so much religious rhetoric that befogs our atmosphere. But an episode out of my past illustrates this vividly. Jim and I were in the university together; I was an undergraduate student committed to the ministry, and he was finishing his first graduate degree in physics. He had a sharp intellect and a compulsion to find out what things meant that seemed to intimidate even some of his professors. And Jim's relentless pursuit for truth penetrated every area of his life, including the church.

I can still remember the Sunday when our Bible teacher, a sharp businessman who had been enlisted to teach a college men's class, finished his little presentation on "Putting God First." Since there was still some time left, he asked for questions or discussion. Normally, in many classes this would just have opened the way for a replay of Saturday's football game. But I can still see the amazement on Mr. Breen's face when Jim said, "I think the phrase 'putting God first' is too abstract and needs to be fleshed out and applied if it is to make any sense. Would you tell me exactly how I put God first. What do I need to believe, decide, feel, or do?" Fortunately, the dismissal bell rescued Mr. Breen, but the question stuck in my mind, and I have been working on the answer ever since.

It seems to me that if we are to put God first, we must at the same time accept the fact that his plan for our lives has top priority over any that we might have. An acceptance of this truth will drive us to persistently seek his guidance for every part of life. This, of course, is scary because there is always risk involved in turning our lives over to someone else. But the act of doing this actually shifts the control from ourselves to God. And while on the surface this might seem risky, on a much deeper level it creates a new focus for our lives and enables us to deal with our fears from a stronger base.

I had never met Zelma personally, but she saw my name in a *Guideposts* magazine in her dentist's office in Lexington, Kentucky, and decided from the article I had written that I might be able to help her. She got my number from the information operator and called me at home on a Saturday afternoon. Zelma was a very frightened woman, and as I listened, she poured out her anxieties about her marriage which was under strain, about tensions with her father, about confrontation with her teenage children, and about her fear that some surgery she was facing might be more serious than the doctor had really indicated. There was a desperate "please tell me something I can do" quality to her whole conversation.

After listening carefully, I said, "Look, Zelma, I'm so far away and you need someone close by. I have a very good minister friend who just moved to Lexington, and I know he will be willing to help you if you ask him." I gave her his name and suggested she might want to visit his church, introduce herself to him, and ask for an appointment to see him. She seemed delighted at the idea of possible help closer to home and assured me she would do what I suggested.

Three weeks later I got a letter from the pastor thanking me for sending Zelma to him. He had met with her several times, had gotten to know her husband and children, and was able to help her make a decision which gave God priority in her life. During that short period of time she and her husband had joined the church and had begun to involve their children in some of the youth activities. Then a week later I got a call at the office from Zelma telling me about all that had happened and thanking me for finding her some friends in her own hometown. She sounded like a different person from the one I'd talked to before. Her voice resonated with laughter and hope and confidence. But the most exciting news of all came through when she said, "Making the commitment I did to God didn't take away my problems, but it took away the fear. I can't explain it, but when I look at them now, they don't seem so unmanageable."

A second principle Jesus gave in the Sermon on the Mount which helps us manage fear and anxiety is: *learn to live in the present.* He states the point negatively: "Do not be anxious about tomorrow, for tomorrow will care for itself. Each day has enough trouble for its own." (Matt. 6:34, NASB). This is not counsel to either abandon the lessons of history or ignore the demands of the future. Rather, we are to focus our lives in the present tense. It is a warning against loading down our today with the regrets of yesterday and the uncertainties of tomorrow. This idea was graphically noted by my eighth grade teacher on the blackboard one day. There for all of us to see and think about were these words, "Yesterday is a cancelled check, tomorrow is a promissory note, today is all I have to spend." I didn't realize at the time how hard it is to live a day at a time, and I've learned since how much fear and anxiety is generated when we don't.

The two worst enemies of living in the present are questions and statements that begin with "What if . . . ?" and "If only . . ." The first question turns our imagination loose to explore all the uncertainties of the future. *What if* my grades don't qualify me for med school? *What if* I go to the doctor and he finds a tumor? *What if* I retire and don't have enough money to live on? *What if* our son marries that girl and it doesn't work out? *What if* I lose my job? *What if* I'm left alone? Any one of these questions can create crippling fear.

It's interesting to me that when we are looking to the future we don't usually think about good possibilities. We seldom say what if I graduate Summa Cum Laude and have my pick of med schools?; what if I go to the doctor and he says, "You're the picture of health"?; what if our son's marriage makes them both very happy?; what if I'm president of the company?; what if we both live to celebrate our sixtieth wedding anniversary? There is something about using up today's energy by looking at tomorrow which makes us afraid. This is why we need to learn to live in the present.

The statements beginning "If only . . ." turn our memories loose to replay all our yesterdays, and we tend to do the same thing with the past that we do with the future. We revive our guilt by remembering the wrong we have done; we shame ourselves by remembering the things left undone; we renew our anger by recalling past conflicts; and we discourage ourselves by remembering past failures. While good memories of the past strengthen us, we often dissipate the energies of our todays and fill our lives with anxieties which erode our joy by trying to relive yesterday in our minds. The poignant line in John Greenleaf Whittier's poem entitled "Maud Muller" continues to speak to us:

> Of all sad words of tongue or pen,
> The saddest are these: *"It might have been!"*

Our "might have beens," though, can be turned into exhilarating experiences as we confront each day with excitement and commitment, grateful that we have work to do that absorbs our energy and relationships to enjoy that enrich our lives. There is an energy-releasing routine which can set a positive mood for each new day—one I recommend trying. It is deceptively simple but very powerful. At the beginning of each day repeat several times, "This is the day which the Lord has made; let us rejoice and be glad in it" (Ps. 118:24). Living in the present puts both our yesterdays and our tomorrows in a perspective where they don't seem so formidable and full of fear to us. In the good experiences of today, we find a wonderful promise about tomorrow and a kind word of release from yesterday.

The third principle Jesus gave for dealing with fears is: *use common sense in thinking about your fears.* One of the traps we Christians often fall into is being afraid to use the minds which God has given us. We tend to forget the instructions to love him with our *minds* as well as our hearts. It was obvious that when the Apostle Paul was writing to his young protégé Timothy that he was, in places, responding to previously expressed anxieties and fears. Among other things Timothy was apparently struggling with feelings of insecurity concerning his ability to measure up to the responsibilities of life. But in the second letter, after reminding him of the blessing of his rich heritage and of the capabilities God had given him—all of which should have given him confidence and banished his fears—Paul unloaded an absolutely electric statement, "For God hath not given us the spirit of fear; but of power, and of love, and of a sound mind" (2 Tim. 1:7, KJV). That statement is powerful, and we, like Timothy, can unmask our fears as we confront them with our minds and not our feelings.

When Jesus talked to people about their fears and concerns, he urged them to stop being full of anxiety and called their attention to the birds flying around up above. He pointed out that the birds didn't "sow or reap," yet they were cared for, and then he assured his listeners that they were worth more than the birds. It was this kind of thinking which helped them see that God has given us a precise order for the universe and a marvelous support system. And we are able to draw on these enormous resources not only with our hearts and feelings, but with our minds.

Verbalize Your Fears

Fear is often easier to deal with if it can be verbalized. Frequently, when I'm having to handle a certain fear and I'm alone, I take pencil and paper and try to put into words exactly what it is that's causing me to be afraid. This is not any easy exercise because so often our fears are really based on rather vague feelings. But I've found that when I persist until I've been able to spell it all out clearly, my fear is easier to handle.

Another therapeutic way to verbalize our fears is out loud to someone who cares for us. I can think of a number of people who across the years have let me work on my fears in their presence. It is good therapy for me to discuss my fears with a close friend, and usually the mere act of doing this frees me to do what is necessary about them.

At the same time I've tried to be a listening friend to other people as they have struggled through their fears and concerns.

Concentrate on Solutions

In most situations we can better concentrate our energies on possible solutions than focusing on our fears. As we ask, "What are the facts?", "What are the alternatives as I see them?", "Who might know of alternatives that I'm not thinking of?" we begin to move toward the unequalled confidence of Paul when he wrote, "I can do all things through Christ which strengtheneth me" (Phil. 4:13 KJV). The "can do" philosophy is not a modern invention. Rather, it is as old as thinking Christians.

Recently I watched three women combine their resources to help a friend who had a larger load than she could carry and whose anxieties about the problems were about to immobilize her. Dorothy, who is an attractive and creative woman, had been seriously ill and really didn't have the strength to care for herself. But she faced the upcoming wedding of her only daughter and the task of finding affordable hospital-nursing care for her elderly mother. It was the problem with her mother that seemed insurmountable to Dorothy, and she just collapsed with a sense of utter helplessness and defeat.

It was at this point that three of her good friends became alarmed and came to see me. As the four of us discussed Dorothy's problem, there just didn't seem to be any solutions that came to our minds. This was a terribly frustrating time because each of us was anxious to help. After an hour or so, we began to see that we needed to draw help from other people who might have ideas which hadn't occurred to us. So a list was made, and the three ladies moved out into their crusade by contacting each of the persons on our list and sharing Dorothy's problem with them.

In slightly more than a week Dorothy's mother had been placed where she would get the care she needed. During that week I talked almost daily with the three friends, and it was exciting to watch what making a commitment to a friend did for them. I forget now which one of the ladies made the following comment, but it greatly influenced my thinking about dealing with fear, "Once we came to the conclusion that there had to be a solution to the problem and made a commitment to find it, it was uncanny how many doors opened to us, and how everyone we made contact with was so anxious to help us find a way."

7

Don't Waste Your Troubles

MY FASCINATION WITH Howard Lee began at Dean Couch's beach house on Galveston Bay on a fall Saturday afternoon when more than a hundred single adults from our church were having a picnic. Howard, who had arranged with his friend Dean for the use of the place, was our unofficial host for the event.

During the afternoon everyone had quite naturally drifted into interest groups—some were crabbing from the long pier, others absorbed the afternoon sun along the seawall, and a few dedicated football fans clustered around a radio, intent on the play-by-play action of two top teams in the Southwest Conference. Those with sensitive skin and no sunscreen were inside reading, and the rest were bunched around a noisy game of horseshoes where Howard Lee and his partner were systematically beating everyone who had the courage to challenge them.

While I have no skill at the game, I remembered, as

a little boy, watching my father pitch horseshoes, so I edged into this group because everyone seemed to be enjoying themselves. I hadn't been watching long until I became intrigued with the way Howard's partner seemed to coach him. After Howard had thrown the first shoe his partner would say, "Howard, you're about six inches to the right and a foot short." The next shoe usually hit the post, and if it wasn't a ringer, it at least scored a point.

This went on until the cooks rang the dinner bell, and as the group broke to get in line for the barbeque, I heard someone say almost to himself, "The only way they will ever beat Howard is to point him in the wrong direction." That's how I found out what everyone else there already knew—Howard is legally blind.

I thought back to earlier in the afternoon when Howard had taken all of us on a tour of the house and grounds and then out on the long pier where the *Princess Patsy I* was tied. The thought never entered my mind that he was not really seeing everything he pointed out to us. On the way back from the end of the pier he'd walked beside me and thanked me for coming. He went on then to give me some background on our host, and talked to me about his interests in the church. His warmth, his love of people, his unselfish spirit were all obvious, but I hadn't picked up a single clue of his vision impairment.

I worked it so I was close to the person in the barbeque line whose comment had tipped me off to Howard's blindness, and when our plates were full, I sat next to him. "I really find it hard to believe he can't see," I confessed, "because he functions like a sighted person."

"He hasn't always been blind," the friend said. "Five years ago Howard's world caved in on him. He had a lovely wife and two grown children whom he loved. After years of work as a lawyer he had built an outstanding practice and was considered by many to be one of the best title men in the city. He was at the peak of his career and his life when within a period of twenty-four months he lost his wife to cancer and his sight to an infection which left him blind." As the friend got up to get some dessert, he dropped an evocative comment that has stayed with me, "It's great to see someone who hasn't let his troubles get him down."

Since then I've spent ten years getting to know and love and admire Howard Lee, and if I were making a list of people who have built successful lives, his name would always be on it. We've talked about the things that have happened to him, and, of course, he has been affected by them. But Howard was able to salvage some qualities out of all the loss and grief and pain and frustration which have brought a richness and fullness to his life he might not otherwise have experienced.

Do Not Waste Your Trouble

The successful person is one who comes to understand that difficulties and trouble are inevitable experiences with all of us as we seek to grow and mature. It is interesting, though, to find, even today, so many sophomoric Christians who refuse to admit that life is not just one victory piled on top of another. When I was a teenager, intoxicated with a rather naïve picture of life, I came across Job's rather bleak comment, "Man is born to trouble as the sparks fly upward" (Job 5:7). That seemed unreal to me, and I decided that he was probably just discouraged at the moment—after all, Christians aren't supposed to have serious troubles! But my more mature thinking tells me just how deceptive that attitude can be. A trouble-free life is a wispy illusion, cultivated in part by the way we try to hide and deny our problems.

Years ago there was a popular song with the not-so-unique theme of a person who had broken up with his true-love and was hurting terribly, but he didn't want anyone to know. The words, "Laughing on the outside, crying on the inside," told the story, and the emotion behind that song describes so well the instinct to hide our troubles from other people. It is possible, I believe, that one of the reasons we are so reluctant to be open and honest with others about our problems and difficulties is that we are unique. We think no one else has problems like ours!

However, when we look just beneath the surface of life, we find that every person ultimately experiences heartache, pain, failure, loss, reversals, frustration, and disappointment. Our natural temptation is to protest against the injustice of such times, "How could a loving God let that happen?" But in reality, that is a myopic view of life, for we know in our better moments that it is out of the tough and sometimes hurtful nitty gritty of life that real flesh and blood persons emerge—persons like each of us who laugh and cry, who draw sudden strength from our successes and are plunged into despair by our failures, but who are always striving to cope with the realities of life.

In my vocation as a minister I have experiences each week which remind me of just how prevalent trouble is in all of our lives. For almost ten years now I have been the pastor of the same congregation in Houston. During this time our lives have been woven together in literally hundreds of shared experiences, great and small, joyous and sad, social and ceremonial. We have played together, planned together, argued with each other, worked for common causes, studied and worshiped, and served together. Consequently, when I preach on Sunday morning, I'm not delivering a neatly put religious essay to strangers. Rather, I'm sharing from my own experiences and from God's Word with people whom I know and love.

Frequently, while listening to the anthem which precedes my sermon, I will look at the people in each pew and recall the burdens and the hurts which I know they are wrestling with on this particular morning. A visitor with an untrained eye might look around this well-dressed, smiling, and attentive congregation and assume that they didn't have a worry in the world. But I know them, and I see persons with deep concerns about health, job, family, relationships, and finances.

Out there is a beautiful family whose life is being reoriented by a stroke the father suffered which made him unable to continue his career . . . a recent widower who is so lonely he can hardly stand it, and he can't seem to communicate this to his children . . . a staff member who will go from the church to visit her mother in a rest home, knowing that she probably won't even be recognized . . . a middle aged woman who cared for her mother over twenty-five years, and this is her first time to be in church since her death . . . a businessman whose reversals have him on the brink of bankruptcy, but he dreads telling his wife about their desperate situation. And for all the troubles I am aware of, I know these represent only the tip of the iceberg.

Troubles Are Not Punishment for Wrong-Doing

The troubles and difficulties of life have the potential for destroying our happiness, for undermining our effectiveness, and for spoiling our spirits. But one of the most tragic and devastating notions that can assail us during times of trouble is the idea that these happen as punishment for something we have done wrong. The Old Testament story of Job gives us a classic example of this kind of twisted thinking. Tragedy had struck Job's home with a vengeance—his seven sons and three daughters were killed, and he was completely wiped out financially.

When three of Job's friends heard about the tragedy, they hurried over to the house to commiserate with him. But the first suggestion they made was that he had done something wrong and God was punishing him for his sins. What gross insensitivity! And yet, while those friends of Job have been gone for a long time, there seems to be a taint of their philosophy in each of us. Down deep inside we feel surprise—and sometimes outrage—when good people are afflicted with trouble and tragedy. Somehow we have fallen prey to the mistaken notion that a kind of exemption from pain and tragedy and death is created when we worship God and seek to live good lives. If we were asked directly, "Do you think going to church will prevent you from having cancer?" we would give an immediate negative response. But when one of the finest people we know, without any warning, dies of a heart attack, our first instinct is to wonder why this would happen to such a good person. It seems that the philosophy of Job's friends is woven into the fabric of our humanness, but the idea that our troubles come as punishment is as wrong now as it was then.

While it is true, I believe, that events and circumstances are subject to cause-and-effect in our relationship with God, it cannot explain all the bad things which happen to us. Long ago Jesus illustrated that when his disciples asked him whether a certain man was born blind because of his own sin or his parents' sin. Jesus replied, "Neither." And yet there lingers in our consciousness a tendency to add to our troubles by feeling false guilt about them.

No Time for Self-Pity

Trouble is damaging to us as persons when we allow waves of self-pity to flood our thoughts. This truth came alive for me in my late teens when I suffered an almost terminal case of self-pity. Between my junior and senior years in high school I began to have pain and swelling in the ball-joints of my little toes, and when I went to the doctor, he gave me some candy-coated aspirin and said that if I didn't take care of myself I would be crippled by a rheumatic ailment. He suggested that I quit my job and get more rest. But since the fifty-four hours a week I worked in addition to attending school provided much-needed income for my family, it didn't seem possible. But within a few months I was crippled so badly that I was not able to either work or attend school. We were too poor for me to get regular medical help, but eventually I qualified for admission into a state operated crippled children's hospital.

My Uncle Doc took me to Oklahoma City for my appointment with the doctors. It was my first experience in a clinic run by a teaching hospital connected to a medical school, and I was overwhelmed by the two days of tests and what seemed like endless interviews and examinations. The prognosis was rheumatoid arthritis, and they checked me into a ward of the Crippled Children's Hospital with a dozen other teenage boys with different problems. This was a totally new experience for me, and although it occurred over thirty-five years ago, I can still remember how alone and frightened I felt. I thought of my friends and the good time they were having while I was in the scary hospital, and I began to have a very bad case of self-pity.

During my second week at the hospital I had an experience which helped me see what I was doing to myself by my negative attitude. The treatment in vogue for rheumatoid arthritis at that time was a high protein diet, large doses of brewer's yeast and ascorbic acid, plus daily shots of "gold," the shorthand term for gold-sodium-thisulfate. Since the gold had to be given intravenously, the nurse and I became well acquainted and I let some of my steam off in her direction. This had been going on for about a week when I asked her, "Have you ever nursed anyone who had arthritis as bad as mine?" I was sort of desperate for a little sympathy and encouragement. She gave me neither, "I've had one other patient just like you." That was it—nothing more. But I was curious about my fellow-sufferer and how he was getting along. So I said, "What happened to him?" She unwrapped the rubber tourniquet from my arm, placed the syringe and needle in the tray to be cleaned, and picked up my chart to record the shot without seeming to have heard my question. But as she turned to go she looked at me with just the twist of a grin on her mouth and jokingly said, "He died," and walked out of the ward. I decided at that moment that feeling sorry for myself didn't solve any problems and probably just created new ones that I didn't need.

Troubles Need Not Infect All of Life

It is particularly destructive, to allow a problem or a difficulty in one area of our life to infect all of the rest. Even though we are an integrated unity, I believe it is possible for us to function creatively in one part of life while hurting terribly in another.

My friends Ned and Louise were active in the affairs of their college town and were committed to the church where they taught classes of young adults. They had one child, a daughter named Leslie, who seemed destined to copy the best traits of both of her parents. When it was time for Leslie to go to college, she decided not to attend the school in her hometown but applied to the larger, more prestigious, and socially active state university. No one was really surprised at her decision because a large part of the excitement of getting an education seems to revolve around leaving home and going off to school somewhere else.

It wasn't long before her parents and friends could see that something was radically different. It seems that Leslie had made her important friendships with "non-students" who had long ago quit attending classes but still hung around the university. She moved fairly quickly into the drug scene and lost all interest in her classes. Somehow, she managed to stay off probation the first semester, but halfway through her second semester Ned and Louise received word from the university that Leslie was no longer enrolled in school and had moved out of the dorm. They searched frantically for almost a week before finding her. She was alone and ill and depressed, so they took her home, but there was little communication because Leslie had withdrawn and spent hours just staring blankly out of the window. The doctor who saw her regularly said it would take months to begin dealing with all that she had been through.

Ned and Louise were devastated by what had happened, but their friends in the community and the church rallied to them with love and understanding and their prayers. But they seemed unable to respond, and I was shocked one day when Ned said to me, "Kenneth, I've got to resign from the Sunday school class I'm teaching. I feel like a hypocrite trying to lead young adults when I've made such a mess of my own life."

It seemed clear that Ned and Louise had lost their sense of self-esteem and self-worth. They blamed themselves for Leslie's behavior and then allowed their feelings of failure to take over and discolor all of life. None of us will escape times of heart-wrenching difficulties and trial . . . we experience times of intense hurt, but we, during those periods, must not allow ourselves to be crippled emotionally. Rather, our best therapy is to continue doing those things we do well. In fact, many of the momentous achievements and discoveries which have revolutionized our thought and lifestyle have been accomplished by people who in certain parts of their lives were experiencing excruciating trouble.

One of America's favorite radio and television personalities for many years has been Art Linkletter. At the time of the drug related tragedy with his daughter, Mr. Linkletter handled his great pain by speaking across the country to parents and teenagers with drug problems. Franklin D. Roosevelt was president during my entire youth and was able to give leadership to the country during a critical time of its history even though he had been crippled by polio after coming to adulthood. Beethoven continued to compose even after the loss of hearing made it impossible for him to hear the music he was writing. And although he suffered from what he called his "thorn in the flesh," the Apostle Paul became the human instrument for the writing of half of the New Testament. Most of the successful people I have known personally or have read about had to function in spite of pain and tragedy in their lives.

David's Response to Trouble and Broken Dreams

Several years ago I made a discovery, almost accidentally, which has given me a whole new way of looking at and handling the difficult experiences and the down periods of my life. It was early fall, and I was mapping out an in-depth study of the Old Testament character David in preparation for ten or twelve sermons in the spring. Obviously, between the account of David's life and the Psalms, there is an abundance of stories and material on David. Because of this I needed to be very selective about what I should use and the direction these sermons should take. And right at the outset I decided to bypass the only two events in his life which most people know about—that he killed a giant named Goliath with his sling-shot and that he had an affair with a married woman named Bathsheba.

Now I already knew a lot about David, but I decided to carefully study his life and lift from it those experiences he had with which most of us, even today, could identify. I wanted to learn how to better cope with today's difficulties and problems by discovering just how David handled similar trouble in his day. For example, I learned about David's inability to cope with grief when he was immobilized by his son Absalom's death. And I lived with David through the death of his life-dream as he suffered the bitter disappointment when told by God's messenger that he would not be allowed to build the temple on Mount Zion. There is nothing more shattering than broken dreams, but David refused to waste his trouble.

As the days passed, my study of David's life produced new and exciting discoveries. Among these was the explosion of the myth that David just moved from one success to another. It is true that in his early boyhood the prophet Samuel selected him above all his older brothers to be anointed as the future king to succeed Saul. It is also true that when young David visited his brothers in Saul's army which was in battle position in the Elah valley, it was he who had the nerve to take on Goliath when everyone else was paralyzed with fear of the Philistine giant. Things continued to break well for him when he moved into the king's palace and became intimate friends with Prince Jonathan. And from there on he began building a solid reputation as a soldier and an entertainer of the king with his music. David's rise was meteoric.

This apparent success pattern is viewed by many Christians today as their birthright—once God touches our lives, everything, in the long run, will break right for us. We fully expect that we will move from victory to victory without stumbling or falling or facing any formidable obstacles. This hollow notion is even palmed off on unsuspecting people by many ministers. Over the years, and without being aware of it, I had unconsciously bought into at least some of that sort of thinking. But my close look at *all* of David's life opened my eyes to something I had never seen before—"the pasture-to-palace-without-pain" idea leaves out two long and significant periods of David's life which stand in stark contrast to the others. I discovered that before David actually became king he spent several years as a fugitive. Because of David's popularity Saul became insanely jealous of him, and he escaped from the palace and went into hiding in fear of his life. For several years Saul, with David on his "most wanted list," tried to track him down and kill him—almost one-third of the book of 1 Samuel is devoted to this time. Finally, David concluded that if he stayed in Israel, Saul would eventually get him, so with several hundred men, his insurgent army, he escaped across the border and became an exile in Philistia.

This intriguing period in David's life when he was on the run and was hunted like an animal raised a question in my mind: what part did these seemingly "down" years play in the development of God's purpose for his life? Was it just a time for treading water while he waited for the climactic moment when he would take over as king? Were these wasted years?

I suppose one of the most difficult and at times painful ideas we wrestle with is that there is no need for any of our experiences to be wasted. In partnership with God, every circumstance can become a positive force in our march toward maturity and fulfillment. It seems to me this was true of David's dark years as a fugitive—God was preparing him to assume the responsibilities as the leader of a great nation. Even his time of exile in a foreign country quite likely broadened his vision and expanded his sense of purpose, for I could see a tremendous change in the David who was installed as King of Israel at Hebron and the David who fled the palace in fear of Saul years before. A young idealist had run from the palace, but a king emerged from the wilderness to take command. Israel needed to be politically united, to build alliances with other powers, to unify her religion, and to move from a posture of survival to one of mission—David was ready.

Lessons from David

There are a lot of lessons for each of us in the experiences of David. We learn that times of difficulty can become significant moments of preparation for leadership. So often we see where a lonely "wilderness experience" became a powerful influence in preparing so many of the people written about in the Bible for their times of effectiveness. Such moments of isolation and aloneness cause us to see only the downside of life. David certainly experienced the devastating feeling that, in the midst of his trouble, God had forgotten all about him: "How long, O Lord? Wilt thou forget me for ever? How long wilt thou hide thy face from me?" (Ps. 13:1). And when he was hiding in the caves as a fugitive with only a handful of faithful men, he said: "Preserve me, O God, for in thee I take refuge, I say to the Lord, 'Thou art my Lord; I have no good apart from thee' " (Ps. 16:1–2).

It was out of those times of spiritual and emotional desolation that David's faith matured and he was prepared for his great moments. None of his troubles had been wasted.

It was during the time I was studying the life of David that I preached a sermon one Sunday morning entitled, "What to Do with the Down Periods of Your Life." Now, as a rule, members of most congregations are generous and kind in their responses to a minister's sermons. But I wasn't prepared at all for the reactions on this one.

Apparently, I had touched a hot button with most of the people who heard me that morning. I was deluged for several weeks by telephone calls, notes, and personal conversations. The heart of much that was said is best expressed in the honest words of one person, "Pastor, that was a nice talk about David and his problems, but all of that happened so long ago. I find it hard to believe that what I went through when my husband left and what I'm going through right now with my children can possibly be of any good in my life. It seems like everything is downhill." This lady, like most of the people who had heard me, seemed to feel that one way or another her particular hurt or need was outside God's ability to keep it from destroying her.

I can understand their feeling, because my own spiritual pilgrimage has frequently been rocked by my efforts to find answers. It seems to me that during the years I've been a Christian I have been exposed to a longer list of weak explanations of trouble than Job's friends would have ever thought up. I sometimes wish I had kept a journal which listed in detail the many ludicrous explanations I've heard for the trouble and difficulties we all experience. And, tragically, many of these came from folk with Bibles in their hands and an ultra-pious tone of voice. So frequently we tend to accept at face value what is said under those circumstances. But I know that as the years passed in my own search for truth, I had to drop a lot of pitifully inadequate notions about how God relates to and treats people in all circumstances of their lives. And I can now be absolutely certain about one thing—there is nothing that can happen to any of us that is outside of or beyond God's ability to relate it to his purpose for our lives.

An Unsolved Puzzle?

I must confess, though, that throughout all of my early struggle to come to an understanding of God's purpose in my life the six words, "All things work together for good," remained an unsolved puzzle to me. The phrase comes from the Apostle Paul's letter to the Romans, and the entire verse reads: "And we know that all things work together for good to them that love God, to them who are the called according to his purpose" (Rom. 8:28 KJV).

Now, if those words had come from a Greek philosopher or an English poet, I would have rejected them as not being true, but they were from the Word of God. I can recall sitting at the funeral of a child who had died in a tragic accident; the minister's text for the funeral service was "All things work together for good." I can still recall the anger building up in me as I looked first at the anguished parents in such need of comfort and then at the well-meaning minister who was forcing them to view their loss with a kind of loveless fatalism and was asking them to respond to it with a deadening resignation. As I sat there obsessed with an unexpressed fury, I said over and over to myself, "There must be a better understanding of those words."

It was at this time that out of the agony of my mind I began slowly to arrive at what for me is a reassuring interpretation of these words and one of the most helpful insights in the Bible.

I first began to see that these words *do not* teach that everything which happens to us is good. There are a lot of things which happen to us that are not good, and we certainly don't help the situation by pretending that they are. Paul knew this—in one place he gives a long list of some of the bad things that had happened to him, (2 Cor. 11:23–28). He had suffered hatred and violence more than once. Paul experienced betrayal by people he trusted. Years of his life were seemingly wasted in jail. He suffered recurring illness, and his health was ravaged by the rigors of his extensive travel. Paul's "all things work together for good" was never intended to suggest that all that happens to us is good. And I came to see that in a world full of disease and violence and stress a lot of bad things can happen, and some of them are going to happen to me and to those I love.

Then I also came to see that God does not *purpose* these adverse things that happen; it is not his intention for our lives. And I always cringe when well-meaning people tell someone who has a malignancy or has lost a child in death or has gotten fired from a job or has suffered the devastation of a broken marriage, that it is God's will. Dr. E. Stanley Jones, distinguished missionary of a generation or two ago helped me to see the kind of emotional and spiritual schizophrenia that is created by this kind of defective thinking when he recalled a grief experience he shared with a colleague in India whose child had died suddenly. As Jones tried to comfort his friend, he was told by the grieving father, "I guess this is what God wanted." Jones was horrified by what his friend was doing to himself with this kind of thinking, so he said to the friend, "What if I told you that God had nothing to do with your daughter's death? What if you were to learn that someone slipped into her room at night and placed a piece of cotton saturated with bacteria right close to her nose where she would breathe the contaminated air? How would you feel about that?" Immediately the man's face became twisted with the inner rage that surged through him, and he said, "If that had happened, I would spend all the energies of my life finding the person who did it, and I would kill him with these two hands." The point was made; Jones didn't have to ask, "Then why aren't you mad at God?"

As we read the Old Testament, we discover that the

people of ancient Israel were so frightened at the danger of "other gods" that they saw God as the source of evil as well as good. Modern Islam still has a view of the cause of events which is almost completely fatalistic. It basically concludes that whatever happens is what God wants to happen and that the only way to be happy is to accept the "will of Allah" without complaint.

On the other hand, the Christian believes in a sovereign God of power—a moral, purposeful, loving, caring God and not a cold, vengeful, impersonal being. Our God is the enemy of lies, of violence, of death, of tears, and of everything that thwarts his purpose for us.

A Different Perspective

It wasn't until I got rid of the heinous idea that everything which happens to us is God's will that I began to understand the true meaning of Paul's words, "All things work together for good." I believe these verses tell us that God is not going to abandon us in our troubles, but will work with us to transform what has happened to us. A more literal translation of Paul's words is, "We know that in everything God works for good with those who love him" (Rom. 8:28). This gives these words an entirely different perspective from the way I heard them being used before. It means that if we turn to God in the midst of our trouble he will begin there to work with us to salvage some good out of the bad. In most cases we will never know why certain things happen to us or to others, but we get a very clear picture that we ought to bring our trouble, whatever it is, to God and ask him to help us salvage good from it.

This is really the principle of Christ's death on the cross at work in our lives. Who would say that from the human point of view the events which led to Christ's death were good? It was a picture of intrigue, betrayal, compromise, ambition, and violence. Crucifixion was the most contemptible form of death ever devised. Yet today the cross is a symbol of hope, not because it was good to begin with, but because God's power took what was bad and made it good. This, then, is the whole concept of Christian conversion. When our lives fall short of the ideal, we are not abandoned but are still loved, and God continues to work with us. If we let him, God is able to come to us in the midst of our trials and problems and work his purpose in our lives so that what has happened does not thwart it. God's transcending purpose need not be frustrated by the troubles we have if we turn to him with them. I've watched this principle at work in the lives of people in small matters and large, and I have never seen it fail.

God is always able to salvage some good from the troubles we have if we let him. Recently, I spent a Monday with our daughter Nancy who is a student at the University of Michigan Law School in Ann Arbor. The doctor told her that it would be wise to remove and test a lump he had been observing in her breast for four months. Nancy arranged for the first available appointment. The surgical procedure could be performed with a local anesthetic, so the surgeon suggested that she come to the out-patient clinic.

On the day of her appointment we had breakfast together, arrived at the hospital a little early, and got all the forms completed before the surgical nurse came in to check with Nancy. Then the surgeon came in and discussed exactly what he was going to do, how long it would take, what kind of scar she would have, how much blood she would lose, and the amount of pain she would feel. The most comforting word he had was that they would do a "frozen section" of the mass that was removed and would have a preliminary report on whether it was benign or malignant.

After surgery while Nancy and I were sitting in her room waiting for the report from the doctor, she said, "You know, Daddy, something like this puts things in better perspective in a hurry, doesn't it?" The report was good, and though there was enough pain to require medication, we spent the day in quiet celebration before I went home and she began studying for a final exam she had missed because of the surgery. I came home emotionally and physically exhausted, but out of it had come a closeness to Nancy which will enrich all of our future relationships.

For a long time Edith Schaeffer wrote a column for *Christianity Today* magazine. Her range of subjects was as wide as her considerable interests and deep insights. Sometimes the titles gave clear evidence as to what the subject was, and at other times they were used as interest getters. I almost skipped the one entitled "Sponge Cake or Noodles," and I'm glad now that I didn't, because the story she told illustrates perfectly the point of this chapter.

Mrs. Schaeffer told how one day she gave their cook a recipe for sponge cake only to have her return later with a large bowl of yellow sticky stuff. "Is this what it's suppose to look like?" she asked. One glance told her that something was wrong. "Are you sure that you followed the recipe?" The response was an immediate "Yes," but as they began to check the recipe point by point, the startled and embarrassed cook exclaimed, "Oh, I've left out the sugar. Should I just throw it away and start over?" As Edith Schaeffer looked at that bowl full of good ingredients, she couldn't stand the thought of wasting it, so she said, "Wait just a minute. What do we like that takes eggs, salt, baking powder, flour, and water?" Then with a flash of inspiration she quickly added flour to make the mixture stiff, rolled it thin, cut it into strips, and cooked some egg noodles. Her guests at dinner said those noodles were the best they had ever eaten. Several even asked for a copy of the recipe.

This is how God works with us in spite of our troubles and mistakes. We come to him with missing ingredients and sometimes even the wrong ingredients, but instead of throwing us out he takes what we have and begins to work with it.

Actually, this isn't a new idea. It's exactly the word picture Jeremiah the prophet drew of the potter who was shaping a clay pot on the wheel when something went wrong. But instead of throwing it out the potter molded it successfully into something else. Nothing is ever wasted when we take our troubles to God.

8

Build a Support System for Your Life

AS A CHILD I WAS fascinated by the explorers who did things for the first time, whether they were climbing Mt. Everest or racing for the North or South Pole. To me these men were symbols of individual achievement. I cut their pictures out of newspapers and magazines and saved them. They were heroes—models—that influenced my life during those formative years. I was a grown man, though, before I came to see that their achievements would have been impossible without the help of a large and dedicated team. It was true that a few household names captured the headlines, but their success was largely dependent on a well-organized, complex, and effective support system.

Probably most of us are unwitting victims of the false notion that great achievements are the result of individual effort—that if we try hard enough on our own, we can succeed, without help from others. This is probably a carry-over from our earlier frontier mentality when sort of a rough and ready individuality captured the imagination of an exploding society.

But a thoughtful and below-the-surface look at events then and now assures us of the importance of support. Each of us desperately needs a network of supportive people—people who will love and accept us under any circumstances. I believe that if we are to become the kind of whole and complete persons God has designed us to be, we must draw strength, courage, and insight from supportive family and friends—we cannot make it on our own.

Support from Within Your Family of Origin

The word *family* is broader than most people realize. But it starts with our *family of origin*—with parents and brothers and sisters. Even though my father has been dead almost four years, I still have my mother, two brothers, and two sisters. While we were separated by our parents' divorce when we were still children and have never lived close enough to spend much time together, we've worked at building a family relationship and are learning to lean on each other during good times as well as in times of crisis.

Over the years we have enjoyed our family reunions—several of which were held at my father's farm in southern Indiana. In many people's minds this sort of thing may seem like a relic out of a dim past. But I've come to believe that so many of the feelings of loneliness and alienation that pervade our society today come from our having lost emotional contact with our family of origin. Our roots have been cut and we're adrift somehow. Alex Haley seemed to epitomize the inner longing of people everywhere for contact and relationship with our immediate family of origin as well as with our more distant heritage. His epic best seller, *Roots*, has created a national awareness of family and of roots that will, hopefully, help us recapture a vital link in our emotional and spiritual development.

But, while the good times shared with parents and brothers and sisters have held our family together, it has been our mutual support during periods of crisis that has bonded us into a more caring unit. We were drawn together and gave each other support during the severe medical problems of my brother Charles . . . at the untimely death of my sister Norma's husband . . . and four years ago we shared each other's pain and anxiety as we spent a week together around the deathbed of my father. We drew strength and love from each other that melted away the feelings of separation and distance that come from our living so far apart.

Support from within Your Immediate Family

As a support system, marriage has gotten quite a bit of bad press the last few years. And it is true that the divorce statistics seem to paint a rather gloomy picture—one to one-and-a-half marriages out of three are falling apart under a cloud of frustration and bitterness, and the dissatisfaction among the still-married is distressing.

But at the same time men and women seem to be reaffirming their need for each other with renewed vigor. There is vast evidence beginning to surface that young people have come to see that alternative styles haven't worked, that there is no substitute for the intimate relationship of marriage. It is indeed the deepest and most profound of all human relationships, and one that offers the greatest potential for support available for any two people.

In spite of the macho act, men desperately need to feel the support of their wives. Daily verbal and nonverbal affirmation can do wonders for a man's self-esteem.

I know! For during the twenty-seven years of our marriage my wife Barbara has been liberal not only with her own expressions of support, but at times when I seem to need it the most, she passes along an affirmation or a compliment someone else has paid me.

Scarcely a day goes by that I don't feel the strength of Barbara's support in my professional life. And being a minister's wife is no easy downhill trip. In fact, being the wife of any man irrespective of his vocation is a difficult task. It requires grace and patience and intense commitment—a commitment based not just on feelings of the moment, but on the living reality of a deep love that is also broad enough to cover our differences.

I am thankful, too, for Barbara's support of my avocational interests. Over the years she's been my companion on fishing trips and sailing excursions, and now many of our spare moments are absorbed with a small farm where we're caring for sixteen cows and their calves. It is true each of us has also pursued our individual interests, but successful marriages are built by couples who work constantly to expand their own interests and also work at doing things together.

And, of course, in marriage we are traveling a two-way street. Wives need the daily support and affirmation of their husbands. This is a very sensitive subject. I know, because my boyhood model was not good. My father was not supportive of my mother, and my grandfather had not been supportive of my grandmother. I'm sure both of them would have denied the charge simply because their definition of "support your wife" meant providing for a home and groceries. There was no apparent concern for building a sense of worth or for affirming and applauding their wives' accomplishments.

Because of the fact that I grew up without this kind of a support system in our home, I have at times experienced difficulties in being supportive of Barbara. My tendency—and it is true of far too many men—has been to bury myself in my vocation. While the reasons for a compulsive preoccupation with one's work may sound good on the surface, they are actually superficial and phony. And I've now come to see that my profession, as important as I believe it to be, must not inhibit my relationship with and support of Barbara.

In my case this resolve was tested just recently when I decided not to seek a high office in my denomination. While there were several reasons for my decision, one of the most important to me had to do with my relationship to Barbara. Were I to pursue that position, it would require considerable travel. And since we are just now entering the empty-nest stage of our lives, we want to be able to enjoy these years together in mutual support. For twenty-five years we've had children in the home—now there's just the two of us, and we want to make the most of it.

The support a husband and wife can give each other has the potential to turn a boring and otherwise dull relationship into one of daring adventure—or it can turn a good marriage into a better one. We need to work consciously at it every day of our lives, but the results make it all worth the effort.

There's another form of family support that has been at work in our home in recent years—the support that now exists between our sons and daughters. Like most kids when they were young, they fussed and fought until we thought we'd go out of our minds. But now that they are in three different schools in three different cities, they are drawing closer to each other emotionally. Long letters back and forth and thirty-minute long distance telephone conversations happen frequently. Their conversations and letters range between inane trivia and deadly serious matters. And now and then they even get heavily involved in each other's decisions.

This is an extremely healthy time in their development. They are forming an inner relationship network between themselves and with us that will be supportive wherever they live across the world.

Building a healthy family support system requires the cooperation of each member of the family; however, usually there is one member of the family that takes the lead in making it all happen. Barbara assumes the responsibility for this at our house. She is sensitive to every possible event that deserves a family celebration—birthdays, special holidays, school successes, paying off a loan, just to name a few. Every celebration is treated as a special occasion. And now that all three children are away from home she is already making plans to bring the entire family together once a year.

What works for us won't necessarily fit a pattern for everyone else. But the important thing is to consciously plan what will work for you—and then work the plan.

Support from Your Extended Family

"Family" also means the extended family made up of grandparents, aunts, uncles, and cousins. My parents came from large rural families. This meant, among other things, that as a boy growing up, I had an ample supply of aunts and uncles and cousins to relate to—and *relate* we did! Family vacations with loving relatives were special to this country boy, and today I carry happy memories of those times. I enjoyed them then, but now I see that the love and interaction that flowed between us as a family can be felt even today in the system of values which give my life direction.

The memories which I really treasure have to do with that discovery that I was part of a larger family. Having first cousins to whom I was "related" became very special to me. And I can still recall the feeling I had when Aunt

Lillian told me of the time I had almost died of pneumonia when I was less than two years old. Her remark that evidently God must have had some purpose for my life to have allowed me to live didn't mean much to me then, but I understand it better now.

When I was in my late teens two members of this extended family played pivotal roles in giving support to my life. When the doctors at the Crippled Children's Hospital in Oklahoma City suggested that I stay off my feet for an extended period and that I go on a very controlled high protein diet, I had no place to go, so my Uncle Walter and Aunt Bertie invited me to stay with them even though they already had a houseful. My aunt spent hours cooking special foods for me on her old wood-burning stove. Uncle Walter spent time listening to me, talking with me, and encouraging me—all with great patience. The attention they paid to me at that critical time in my life endeared them to me in a very special way. I still visit Aunt Bertie whenever I can, and I gain strength through her prayers.

Another very important person in my early life was my mother's brother, James Oscar Smith—a quite imposing name, but everyone called him "Doc." He was a carpenter-farmer-preacher who loved life and enjoyed people. In many ways Uncle Doc played the role of a father to me. He was always sensitive to my physical needs, and he exposed me to college by taking me with him to a conference at Oklahoma Baptist University. It was Uncle Doc who guided me through my decision to become a minister, and he was "family" at my seminary graduation years later. He became my first and most significant model for my life and my ministry. He has been dead for many years, but my approach to so much in life is colored by the values and attitudes Uncle Doc instilled in me as a boy.

As I have reflected on the impact my extended family

has had on me, I've been impressed with the feeling that each of us within our family situations may, without knowing it, be in a position to influence greatly the life of some young person. That is an awesome thought to me and a responsibility I am trying to take seriously. So often, as both relatives and friends, the greatest thing we can do for another person is to make them feel important. And one of the best ways to do this is to listen to them.

The Successful Life Needs the Support of Significant Others

A network of intimate friends and significant people is one of the greatest assets we can have, and any person who has two or three intimate friends with whom he or she can be completely open and transparent is abundantly rich. When Floyd and Harriett Thatcher were doing their interview research in preparation for their book, *Long-Term Marriage,* they discovered that the majority of the people they talked with admitted that they did not have even one person in their lives with whom they felt intimate and with whom they could be completely themselves without fear of judgment. We all need a person or persons in our lives who will be honest with us—someone whom we know and respect, someone who knows us well.

Warren Hultgren, pastor of the First Baptist Church of Tulsa, Oklahoma, has been that kind of a friend to me for many years. We first met at a seminary where I was a professor and he served on the board of trustees. A close friendship was formed then which has survived distance and time. He has become my special confidante when it comes to making major vocational decisions.

Nine years ago three members of the pulpit committee from the South Main Baptist Church, Houston, came to Atlanta to have dinner with Barbara and me and to discuss the possibility of my becoming their pastor. It was a relaxed and enjoyable dinner, but I didn't feel there was the remotest chance I would resign as Director of Evangelism for my denomination to become a pastor. But I did promise to pray about it.

The next morning as I began to organize my day, one of the first things I did was to list the reasons why I shouldn't make a change. But on an impulse I decided to call Warren Hultgren and discuss it with him.

To my amazement his immediate reaction was, "You ought to go to South Main." Sensing my shock, he reeled off the reasons. There was validity to everything he said, but I was especially impressed by his argument about what it would do for my family and me if I became the pastor of a dynamic congregation. And he added that he felt I had the personality and talent that would minister to the needs of the congregation. I was stunned. With penetrating insight he had told me the truth I had not been willing to face. And now I know without any doubt that the past nine years at South Main Baptist Church have been the best years of my life. But I might have missed it except for the advice of my friend.

A close look at the lives of individuals whatever their station in life or how noteworthy their accomplishments will reveal the impact of significant others. When Governor Jimmy Carter was elected President of the United States it was interesting that one of the persons he wanted at his inauguration was a grade school teacher. After a third of a century the impression which she had made upon him was still so fresh in his memory that he wanted her to share his day of triumph. In reading Irving Stone's *Origin,* I was interested to learn the pivotal role which one of Charles Darwin's university professors played in his entire adult life. The touch of special friends in our lives is a gift to be prized.

The Successful Life Needs the Resources of a Personal Faith

Is there a bed-rock of existence upon which we can build a life with a sense of security? Is there a fixed or permanent point of reference from which a person can travel through life with a sense of direction? Is there anyone or anything which can hold together all the diversities and complexities of life and give us a sense of unity and wholeness? Is there any valid basis for distinguishing values and for knowing right and wrong? Is there a way to know what we ought to do with our lives? All of these questions can be answered with a resounding "yes" by those people who have entered into a relationship with God which is personal and real.

The people I know and have observed who are building successful lives have a faith which is making the difference in their attitudes and actions. Faith in God brings a unifying quality to life—a harmony that I believe can and should pervade every aspect of our being. After all, God is the creator of life, and that includes our drives—for food, rest, thirst . . . our drives for companionship, for happy marriages, for sex—too many people today want to park God outside the bedroom door. God is the originator of our emotions, our feelings, but he also is interested in our minds, for entrenched there is the need to know and to ask questions. At the same time, God is equally aware of our social needs—for family, friends, security.

The biblical idea of salvation means to be made whole, or to have all the parts properly related to each other. This fact is beautifully illustrated by my friend Freddie, a talented musician who, until a short time ago, had been one of the town's most celebrated playboys. He had a charming personality, a generous supply of talent, made scads of money, and had pursued a lifestyle totally dedicated to the pursuit of pleasure. Then his grandfather, the idol of his life, died suddenly. While Freddie was sitting in the chapel at the funeral, he decided that nothing in his present life could adequately answer the questions which were being raised by the loss of his grandfather. He began a search that day for something that would fill his emptiness and would give him answers about life. In the days that followed he tried to read the Bible, but just couldn't understand it. So he went to some people he knew were Christians and asked for their help. And they patiently guided him on his first simple step of faith and commitment. A month later, at the front of the sanctuary after a service, he came to tell me what was happening in his life. We were standing by the grand piano when I asked him to put into words what was happening to him. He said, "I'm not too articulate as a new Christian, but let me illustrate it with the piano." He slammed his hands down on the keyboard in a random fashion, and the room was filled with discord. "That's what my life sounded like from the inside before," he said. Then he quickly played several rich, vibrant cords and added, "That's how it sounds inside me now."

A relationship with God can also provide a basis for a personal morality. There has always been a temptation to separate religious fervor and moral seriousness; to let the rituals of religion become a substitute for right living. The Victorian Age for Israel was the first half of the eighth century B.C.; it was a time of stability and prosperity and great religious vigor. But God knew that their religiosity was only a surface ritual and had become a substitute for the elemental principles of loving justice, dealing kindly with the poor, and bringing honesty and integrity into all aspects of life.

An equally attractive temptation for many Christians is to reduce the meaning of faith to a few simple "dos" and "don'ts." The Pharisees of Jesus' day were experts at this sort of legalism—the art of reducing morality to outward conformity while at the same time leaving out the more important matters of the law. A religion that is concerned more about appearances than motives and substance has always created insecure, superficial, judgmental people.

Our whole basis for morality is a personal relationship with God, for it is from him that we get both the direction and the dynamic for our life. We find in God's evaluation of the worth of persons the clue as to how we ought to feel—in his sense of fairness we find a standard for our own actions toward others. His willingness to forgive people is a model for beginning again in relationships, and in his continuing presence in our lives, we begin to find resources for moral living on a practical day-to-day basis.

A personal faith in God creates a healthy tension between us and our culture, it provides a game plan for life, it gives us a sense of sacredness about all of life, and it can give us confident feelings of hope for the present as well as the future. The people I know who are in the process of building successful lives draw support from this relationship in every area of their lives.

To sum up, I believe faith in God introduces a whole new dimension to a life. Frequently, I have lunch with my friend Sam. His friendship has come to mean a great deal to me simply because of the contribution he makes to my life. As Vice President of a major oil field publishing house, Sam is deeply involved in energy-related problems as they impact the lives of people in every country of the world. One day he will be approving a layout for a Chinese edition of their off-shore drilling magazine. The next day he could be planning a barbeque and rodeo for five-hundred foreign dignitaries, and on the following week-end he could be flying to Scotland to speak at a seminar. Most everyone who knows Sam is aware of a quality of life that is a bit rare in the world in which he moves. He has an openness and transparency which is a refreshing contrast to those who are afraid to be candid, and there is an honesty in his dealings that reminds people of the day when a man's word was the equivalent of a contract. But I think one of Sam's main attributes is that he treats everyone with respect. But the motivation for all that Sam is and does is wrapped up in the "secret ingredient" of his life—a genuine and maturing relationship with God.

The Successful Life Needs the Support of a Spiritual Family

One Tuesday I had a board meeting in Dallas at noon. So to save time I decided to fly up and back the same day. And since I had some preparation work to do for my mid-week Bible study, I took three or four of the smaller commentaries on the book of Philippians with me. Counting the waiting time at both ends of the line, plus the forty minutes flying time each way, I figured I'd find time for at least two hours of study. Everything went smoothly on my flight to Dallas, but it was different on my flight home. I was in a center seat in the non-smoking section of a full flight. As soon as we were airborne, I got my books out and began reading and underlining. The man on the aisle said, "Those books aren't about the Bible are they?" And when I assured him they were, he asked, "You don't believe all that stuff do you?" When I told him that I did, he let me know that he thought the Bible was a bunch of fairy tales and that the church was just a crutch for people who were afraid to stand on their own. I kept my comments to a minimum and went right on studying.

But my seat companion evidently just couldn't understand how a grown man who lived in the twentieth century could find meaning in the Bible and in a relationship with the church. So he continued to press me on a variety of subjects—death, world religions, evil and suffering, humanism, etc.—about which he was sure we would differ.

Finally, I decided to introduce a subject about which we were apt to agree—the need every person has for community. Since he was married and had children, I asked him what his "scientific humanist" friends would do if they discovered that his daughter had leukemia. He didn't get the connection, so I asked the question differently. "Mr. Lister, do you have a group of friends who know you and love you and care what happens to you and will give you support in all the experiences of life?" He shook his head from side to side several times and then said, "No, that's one of our weaknesses. We don't create a community for each other."

Now the very thing I had described to him in my question is what today's church is able to provide for everyone who seeks it. The most striking feature of the early church was not its doctrine, its rapid growth, or its apostolic leadership, but the remarkable community which God created. It was a community where people loved each other, shared the common experiences of life, grew together in their understanding, and lived their lives in what Luke describes as "unaffected joy" (Acts 2:46, NEB). When hardships came as a result of discrimination and persecution, it was their love for one another and the practical helps which issued from that love which gave them support and comfort.

When a person with only a casual relationship to the church hears about how the early Christians related to each other, he or she is apt to feel that the early church was different from today's church in the kind of support it can give to its members. But I'm happy to say that I don't look back to those days with any sense of nostalgia because I have come to see that the same quality of fellowship and support can exist even in our late twentieth-century church. But we can't participate in it and enjoy it by sitting placidly in our pew on Sunday morning. Rather, we must move beyond the experience of corporate worship and participate in an intimate and supportive way in the lives—the joys and hurts—of our fellow Christians.

This more focused involvement can take many forms: working on some special committee or project; participating in an on-going study group; or participating in one of the church's outreach ministries. This is how we get to know other church members as persons. It is how we get to know about each other's families, interests, and activities. In this way we begin to develop an interest and love for each other—the foundation for support.

Vernon was elected chairman of a twenty-person committee to seek a new pastor to recommend to the church. The group reflected the diversity of the church in age, interest, experience, and involvement. They met weekly for prayer and discussion, and traveled together for a year. They had their times of agreement and disagreement, but a firm relationship-bond existed between them. When the church called the minister they recommended, they decided to continue to get together occasionally just for fellowship. And even though the committee's official function ended nine years ago, their love and interest and support of each other continues to this day.

Rosemary teaches a class of women whose ages range from the middle forties to the early fifties. She is one of the best Bible students and teachers in the church. The casual observer might think this is the reason for the popularity and effectiveness of the class. But an equally important aspect of the class's life is the quality of support which teacher and pupils provide for the members and their families. They know each other, love each other, and take care of each other in practical ways. It may be sending a card when a member is ill or taking food to the family when one of their group is in the hospital. But all of it expresses a concern for each person. This is how the church gives support.

However large or small a church may be, it's in groups like this where individual interests and needs are being met that the real church can be found. Those looking on from the outside may characterize the activities of these groups as "church work," but whether it's singing in the choir, teaching little children, working with the group which visits out-of-town people in the hospital, serving on a church committee, working with youth, or any one of a host of activities, those in the midst of these groups are building a support system for their lives.

Within the context of the church we can develop the gifts and interests which will enrich our lives. Bob and Alice Ketchand recently moved to Washington, D.C., but they took with them an interest which is already opening many doors. Like a lot of bright young people from good families, the two of them drifted away from the church during their college years. While Bob got his law degree from Harvard, Alice finished the requirements for her C.P.A. Then after Bob's hitch in the Navy, they settled down in Houston where he took a position with a prestigious firm and they started their family. At thirty they had more than reached all their goals with no real sense of satisfaction. One day as they were watching their son Peter play, it occurred to them how differently they were rearing their children from what they had been reared. It was then that they made a definite decision to take another look at the church.

They joined a church whose ministries were mostly designed and administered by the laity. The two of them and their children became a part of the worship and study and fellowship and set about finding what they could do with their gifts and interests. Bob was already donating some time as a lawyer to prison inmates who wanted to file an appeal, but could not afford legal help, when he met Chuck Colson, president of Prison Fellowship who himself had spent time in prison for Watergate-related offenses. The two met when Colson visited Bob's church, and the meeting opened up a whole new idea for him about the needs of ex-offenders. Eventually Bob's church set up a study committee to decide the feasibility of a ministry relating to people who had been in prison, and they asked him to be chairman.

The program which they designed and took to the church was broadened to include everyone who might have been affected by an imprisonment, whether as a parent, child, mate, or friend. The program was called "On the Street"—the inmate's term for being out of prison. From its inception this ministry has been outstanding, and Bob Ketchand has developed an understanding and awareness of that work which is matched by very few.

This spring his firm asked him to take a major promotion and move to their Washington, D.C., office. I talked with him before he gave them his answer and he told me, "Frankly, the only negative thing about the whole move is leaving the church and leaving 'On the Street.' " He decided eventually to move, but when he did, he took with him gifts and interests which had germinated, grown, and come to full bloom in a community which had become a support system for him and his family. And before he had unpacked in his new location, doors were being opened to him to expand that interest further.

So often the jobs which we do for a living leave many areas of interest unsatisfied and many gifts undiscovered and unused. Too much emphasis is placed on what we do for money and too little on what we do avocationally.

One of the ways in which the church gives support is by providing a climate for discovering gifts, and opportunities for developing and using them.

When Ruby and Jeanette first started putting together a ministry to Internationals, neither of them dreamed of the skills and insights which would be called forth or that the need they were attempting to address would someday involve several hundred other women who were willing to find out what they were good at. When Nancy and Dan and I first talked of a seminar for the formerly married, we never dreamed what would be called forth from us in the process of doing it. In affirming and using our gifts and interests the church gives us support.

The Church Can Give Support by Providing an Alternate Peer Group

One of the reasons so many of us fail to live up to some of the dreams we have for our lives is that we find it almost impossible to keep on resisting the kind of pressure we feel from our peers. Most of us like to be liked by those around us and don't find it easy to take ridicule even if it's for something which is important to our lives. I knew four brothers, the Boohers, who joined the Marine Corps together, and because they got up and attended worship on Sunday, their fellow recruits referred to them as the "Booher Sisters." In their thinking, church was for women. The most powerful pressure upon young people to use drugs is peer pressure. The overall society is now so permissive in sexual morality that a person with a clearly defined context for sex will not even be taken seriously. The successful life has to be shaped in the midst of these kinds of pressures. This is an area in which the church can play a helpful role.

Many of the organizations and activities which the church sponsors provide an alternate peer group. It doesn't do away with the pressure coming from the rest of society, but it gathers a group of individuals with some common goals and values and commitments, and they draw strength from each other. When the youth choir has a garage sale to make money for a tour, practices extra hours for months, then spends ten days in Toronto, New York, and New Jersey doing concerts and Bible clubs, they are building up some counterpressures for themselves as they prepare to hit school in the fall. When the three young adult Sunday School departments have a big dress-up dinner and enjoy a fantastic evening of music and fellowship, they are saying to each other, "There are a lot of us who are trying to build strong marriages and healthy families." There are none of us who are so strong that we can function without encouragement from others. This kind of support is a real need—and one the church can meet.

The Church Can Provide Support for You in Times of Crisis

In the chapter on "Don't waste your trouble" we've already dealt with the inevitability of some crisis times in each life. The church has always known how to handle serious illness and death and has developed a style of giving support to those who are in need. But in recent years the church has also learned how to minister to those whose marriages have failed or whose nests are empty or who are caring for aging parents. It's a learning process that's taken place over so many years and in such a variety of ways that I had to look at it through the eyes of a stranger to realize what a remarkable support it really is.

While my father was visiting my brother Charles in

Moline, Illinois, he suffered heart failure. I was at a staff retreat at Galveston when the word came that dad had had an attack, so I left immediately for the airport. By sitting up part of the night in St. Louis, I was able to arrive in Moline early the next morning. Later in the day our two sisters arrived, and we began that lonely vigil at the hospital hoping against hope for him to come out of the coma. We took turns staying at the hospital, partly so we could each get a little rest and partly because the intensive care waiting room was too small for all of us plus the others who were waiting with members of their families. There were no new patients during the week, so the group of us in the waiting room developed a closeness.

There was a pay phone in the waiting room so that incoming calls for any of us could be taken there instead of tying up the nursing station phone. Each day I would get six or eight long distance calls checking on how my father was doing, expressing interest, promising to remember all of us in their prayers, and asking if there were anything they could do at home to help. After this had gone on for several days an elderly gentleman named Virgil who came daily to be with his wife said to me, "Young man, I hope you don't mind my telling you something. You are a most fortunate person to be so far away from your home and yet to have so many people who are thinking about you and your family. I hope you realize how lucky you are." I thanked him for reminding me of the support I had just come to expect from being a part of the church.

The Church Can Provide the Source for Life's Most Meaningful Friendships

On the surface this kind of thinking might seem open to criticism in that it looks like I'm suggesting that people ought to withdraw from the world and make of the church a kind of monastic experience. That would be impossible because people who are full of life and have a sense of mission about their life must live in the world. What I am suggesting is that if you are serious about wanting to build a really successful life, then you will just naturally gravitate toward the largest concentration of people with the same interests.

The son of close friends was a distance runner who had a track scholarship to Rice University. He upset the whole sports community in Houston by transferring to Eugene, Oregon. However, to everyone in the know about distance running, it was a perfectly logical decision because that's where the largest number of America's distance runners were training for the Olympics. He went to Oregon because it was there that he could get the kind of support he needed as he pursued his goals.

Our lives need a support system if we are to succeed. A part of building that life is building the support system to sustain it. If you want to shape a successful life, go where you'll get the most encouragement and help. Go where you will have more motivation to grow and mature. Go where your goals and values can be kept the clearest. Go where they won't abandon you if you try something and fail. Go where there are more models for your life to choose from. If you pick your most meaningful friendships from the people you meet at church, you have improved your chances of a successful life a hundredfold.